HELLO & WELCOME

Unless you are a commuter, travelling by train is one of life's great pleasures, enjoyed by people of all ages. The train is inextricably linked with the development of the modern world and arguably the most civilised form of transport on earth.

Train Traveller is a publication dedicated to narrating and illustrating the exciting experiences and opportunities to be discovered in the world of rail travel. Whether it's moments of nostalgia on a historic steam-hauled service, the novelty of riding one of the many narrow gauge railways or taking in the breathtaking scenery of say, the Canadian Rockies. It could be a high on the thrill of hurtling through the countryside on one of the latest high-speed trains, or simply whiling away the time on a luxury cruise service - no other form of transport delivers such a wide choice of life enhancing experiences - and it's not just for travel writers or celebrities! However, the title was originally published in 2020, in the very week that the first COVID-19 lockdown was announced, and that meant that few people actually got to see the title on the bookshelves, let alone buy it. But the publishers have taken the view that it's too good to miss and this lightly updated edition will be seen far and wide.

How often have you heard the expression 'I love travelling on trains'? Why do people love trains? Here's the thing - travelling by train gives you time to think, time to contemplate, time to relax, time to meet up with and talk to people you may never meet again, time to view and enjoy the passing countryside, time to enjoy a coffee or a meal, time to read a book or listen to some music (through your headphones), you can even sleep on one while it transports you to another destination - and yes, time to prepare for your business meeting - all in relative comfort. And, of course, when you arrive you are in the centre of things - not the periphery. In other words, trains are the ultimate time machine - so I for one understand just why people enjoy trains so much.

We have packed a lot into this publication - with personal accounts of travelling on board trains throughout Europe, Japan, Sri Lanka, New Zealand, Australia, Canada, and the UK. There is a feature on the 1,147mile (1,846km) journey that Amtrak's Cardinal service makes three times a week between New York and Chicago, and we spotlight the breath-taking scenery and abundance of desirable destinations accessible within Wales on its one thousand plus miles of mainline railway and five internationally recognised narrow-gauge railways. And if you have never travelled on a sleeper, a description of the Caledonian service between London and Scotland might just tempt you.

Last but not least, for those of you who love the evocation of railways, past and present and keen to don your boots or Lycra, we have an article about the Railway Ramblers Club and the many picturesque routes in Cornwall where the ghosts of bygone trains can still be summoned. To round all of this up, Michael Williams, a best-selling author and journalist on railways and travel, writes about the romance of railways and the virtues of nostalgia.

Enjoy.

Graham West - editor

BELOW | *One of the joys of Interrail - the opportunity to travel across Italy on the high speed Frecciarossa.*
PIC HITACHI

TRAIN *TRAVELLER* CONTENTS

CONTENTS

6   **THE GRAND TYKE EXPRESS**
Only on a train can you find yourself immersed in a rewarding conversation with complete strangers. Ken Fairfield experienced one such journey.

12   **JAPANESE IF YOU PLEASE**
Think fast and efficient trains and you think of Japan. Carol Longbottom visited and whilst there made train travel one of her highlights.

20   **CINCINNATI'S ICONIC UNION TERMINAL**
Proposals to build a Union Station in Cincinnati aired in the 1890s, but it was 1933 before it opened. John Leddsome chronicles this magnificent building.

26   **THE CARDINAL**
Travelling between New York and Chicago three times a week the Cardinal travels to some of America's most famous states and cities.

30   **SEVEN MILES OF SMILES**
Whatever your age, who can deny the joy and exhilaration of riding on a narrow gauge railway? One such gem is the Lake District's 'La'al Ratty'.

37   **BOOK REVIEW - SETTLE AND CARLISLE RAILWAY**
The Settle and Carlisle line is the subject of this insightful book written by Paul Salveson.

38   **DOWN MEMORY LANE**
There are more than 70 heritage railways in Australia. One of the best is the Kuranda Scenic Railway. Katie Woodhouse and her husband took a ride on it.

45   **BOOK REVIEW - SLOW TRAINS TO ISTANBUL**
Tom Chesshyre delivers a fascinating and thought-provoking commentary on a 4,570 mile journey from London to Istanbul and back - mostly by train!

46   **SLEEP TIGHT**
We look at the all-new Caledonian Sleeper service - a bucket list item for anyone with a love of rail journeys.

52 TROUBLED, EXOTIC SRI LANKA
The luxuriant, tropical island with its palm-fringed beaches, lush green hills and misty mountains has a fine rail network, as John Hart discovered.

60 NOT A TRAIN IN SIGHT
There are hundreds of miles of disused tracks in the UK. Jeff Vinter explains the Railway Ramblers Club and the legacy they have helped create.

66 THE ROCKY MOUNTAINEER
In 1885, Canadian railroad engineers finally linked western and eastern Canada. The Rocky Mountaineer follows the route from Vancouver to Banff.

78 THE JOY OF INTERRAILING – FOR OLDIES!
There is a real sense of adventure when embarking on a long train journey; and the joy of Interrailing is not just for the gap-year generation.

85 BOOK REVIEW – AROUND THE WORLD IN EIGHTY TRAINS
Written by Monisha Rajesh, this book is her account of her modern equivalent of 'the grand tour'.

86 MAGICAL, MYSTICAL WALES
You would struggle to find anywhere else in the United Kingdom, possibly Europe that offers such a diversity of landscape in as small an area as Wales.

94 A HISTORICAL TRAIN OF EVENTS
A tale that links George Pullman to Georges Nagelmackers to Agatha Christie to James Sherwood and to the Belmond Venice-Simplon-Orient Express.

101 BOOK REVIEW – ANGLO SCOTTISH SLEEPERS
The history of the Anglo Scottish sleeper service. One of the last truly romantic experiences left on the mainline railway system in Britain.

102 A SCENIC EXTRAVAGANZA
The line between Auckland and Wellington in New Zealand is listed as the 'North Island main trunk line'. It is anything but a 'trunk line'.

110 ROMANCE OF THE RAILWAYS
Michael Williams has done more train travelling than most and is well placed to understand the romance of the iron road.

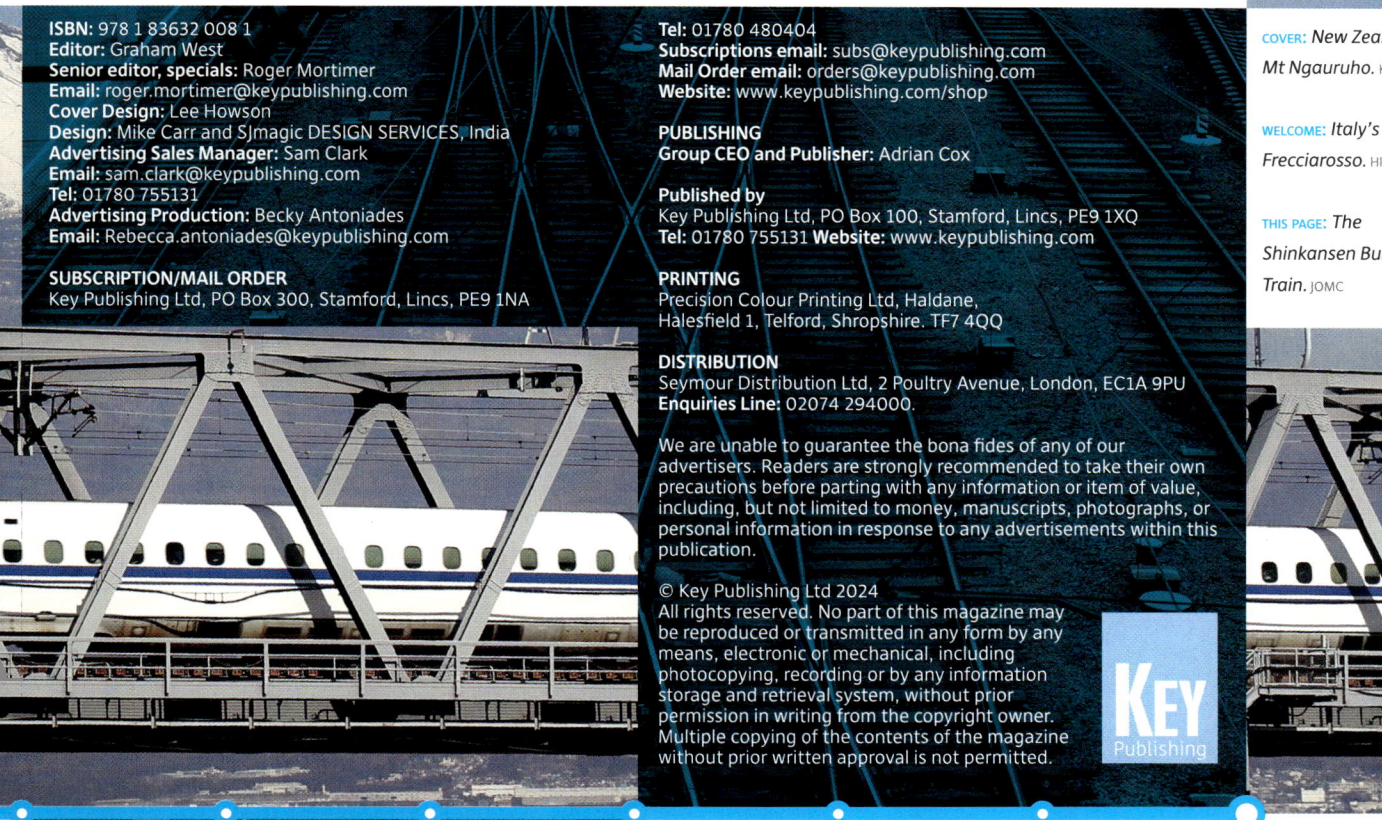

ISBN: 978 1 83632 008 1
Editor: Graham West
Senior editor, specials: Roger Mortimer
Email: roger.mortimer@keypublishing.com
Cover Design: Lee Howson
Design: Mike Carr and SJmagic DESIGN SERVICES, India
Advertising Sales Manager: Sam Clark
Email: sam.clark@keypublishing.com
Tel: 01780 755131
Advertising Production: Becky Antoniades
Email: Rebecca.antoniades@keypublishing.com

SUBSCRIPTION/MAIL ORDER
Key Publishing Ltd, PO Box 300, Stamford, Lincs, PE9 1NA

Tel: 01780 480404
Subscriptions email: subs@keypublishing.com
Mail Order email: orders@keypublishing.com
Website: www.keypublishing.com/shop

PUBLISHING
Group CEO and Publisher: Adrian Cox

Published by
Key Publishing Ltd, PO Box 100, Stamford, Lincs, PE9 1XQ
Tel: 01780 755131 **Website:** www.keypublishing.com

PRINTING
Precision Colour Printing Ltd, Haldane, Halesfield 1, Telford, Shropshire. TF7 4QQ

DISTRIBUTION
Seymour Distribution Ltd, 2 Poultry Avenue, London, EC1A 9PU
Enquiries Line: 02074 294000.

We are unable to guarantee the bona fides of any of our advertisers. Readers are strongly recommended to take their own precautions before parting with any information or item of value, including, but not limited to money, manuscripts, photographs, or personal information in response to any advertisements within this publication.

© Key Publishing Ltd 2024
All rights reserved. No part of this magazine may be reproduced or transmitted in any form by any means, electronic or mechanical, including photocopying, recording or by any information storage and retrieval system, without prior permission in writing from the copyright owner. Multiple copying of the contents of the magazine without prior written approval is not permitted.

COVER: *New Zealand's Mt Ngauruho.* KIWIRAIL

WELCOME: *Italy's Frecciarosso.* HITACHI

THIS PAGE: *The Shinkansen Bullet Train.* JOMC

TRAIN *TRAVELLER* *GREAT BRITAIN*

ONLY ON A TRAIN CAN YOU FIND YOURSELF IMMERSED IN A REWARDING CONVERSATION WITH PEOPLE YOU HAVE, PERHAPS, NEVER MET BEFORE OR ARE EVER LIKELY TO AGAIN. **KEN FAIRFIELD** EXPERIENCED ONE SUCH JOURNEY AND RECALLS THE EXPERIENCE.

LONDON

THE GRAND TYKE EXPRESS

'Anticipation', someone said, 'is half the pleasure'! Sitting in a French style café, located in the main concourse of the magnificent St Pancras international station, I was sipping my coffee while indulging myself in a favourite pastime - people watching. Outside, people were scurrying through the concourse in a myriad of directions, some aiming for the Midland Main Line, some for the underground and some making their way to the departure lounge for an onward journey to one of the more exotic continental destinations via the Eurostar - or maybe just Ashford?

Alas, I was not fortunate enough to be travelling to the continent. Having set out from Halifax to London King's Cross in the early hours of that morning I had completed my business for the day and was idling away my time in St Pancras simply because I find it preferable to King's Cross. Even though the stunning new interior was completed I still feel King's Cross station has more in common with a cattle hall than a welcoming arrivals and departure terminal. St Pancras, on the other hand is, in my opinion, the only station in the UK that successfully projects an air of romance, excitement and promise, a feature mostly lost to an earlier era of train travel.

It was fast approaching time for my journey home to Yorkshire - all I had to do was make the dash to King's Cross station and board the last 'Grand Central' service of the day to Halifax. Feeling tired, thoughts of sleeping through most of the journey home were beginning to permeate my mind.

This particular Grand Central service travels between Bradford and London King's Cross. It should really be called 'The Grand Tyke Express' because its first port of call when heading home is Doncaster, followed by Pontefract, Wakefield, Mirfield, Brighouse, Halifax and finally Bradford. So, you can count on most of its passengers being of Yorkshire origin - and listening to the accents on this train, most would have certainly qualified as Tykes. Even the staff exuded that easy, direct, open friendship Yorkshire people are famous for. This has to be one of the quirkiest and friendliest trains in the land!

ONE SIGNIFICANT DIFFERENCE

My train stood alongside the platform nearest to the new concourse so when it was called I was able to board quickly, find my window seat on the left-hand side of the carriage facing forward across a table and settle down with time to anticipate who my travelling companions might be.

LEFT | *The imposing exterior of St Pancras Station and Hotel.*
ADAM WEST

TRAIN TRAVELLER GREAT BRITAIN

"I prayed I wasn't going to be surrounded by the technology of somebody's mobile office and the paraphernalia that often clutters the tables these days."

ABOVE | *A Grand Central 'Adelante' train passing though South Muskam.* RICHARD CATTON

RIGHT | *A busy St Pancras station concourse.* ADAM WEST

I prayed I wasn't going to be surrounded by the technology of somebody's mobile office and the paraphernalia that often clutters the tables these days, turning them into the equivalent of an untidy, outside broadcast unit. It effectively kills any potential conversation.

At the time of my journey Tom Clift was the managing director of Grand Central and he was responsible for introducing the Bradford/London (Grand Tyke Express) service. Sadly, he died in 2012 shortly after my journey and before taking up a role as managing director of Hull Trains. I believe Grand Central's livery is the smartest of all the train operators in the UK and the interior design of this carriage was particularly tasteful, decorated in silver, lilac and purple. At the far end of the carriage, adjacent to the sliding access door, was a life-size monochrome image of a smiling Marilyn Monroe standing beneath a Grand Central sign. I found this totally agreeable.

As the carriage began to fill, I was pleasantly surprised to discover that my seat-side companion was a young lady, I guess in her 30s - I'll call her Samantha for the benefit of

8 | TRAIN TRAVELLER

LEFT | *Paul Day's magnificent bronze statue 'The Meeting' at St Pancras station.* ADAM WEST

BELOW | *The concourse at King's Cross station.* ADAM WEST

this story - and thankfully she wasn't accompanied by a laptop. A little later two other ladies sat down in the seats facing, I guess they would be in their mid 60s. On the other side of the aisle four other ladies occupied the seats, two of whom were obviously companions to the ladies seated opposite Samantha and me. Facing them and sitting alongside the window was a short, slight lady with a strong Latin American appearance, possibly in her 60s. Later in the journey we were to discover that her name was Marina.

Seated next to Marina, closest to the aisle, was Ivy (another made up name) who, after removing her coat and placing it with her other belongings onto the overhead rack, sat down placing a book on the table with the obvious intention of reading it during the journey. Sadly, her journey was to be short lived. Before the train set off another lady turned up and challenged Ivy for the seat. With looks of perplexed bewilderment both scanned their respective tickets and seat numbers. Strangely, both bore the same seat number. The guard was called. How could two tickets have been issued to two different passengers bearing the same seat number for the same journey, with the same departure time? After scrutiny, the guard confirmed that both tickets were correctly issued but there was one significant difference - Ivy had got the wrong day - she was booked on the same train, same seat for the following day! Looking acutely embarrassed she vacated the booth, quickly retrieved her belongings, and stepped back on to the platform. Hey, it happens.

IMPOLITE EXPLETIVES

The rightful occupant of the seat took her place (I'll call her Mary), sat down and immediately buried her head in a book trying hard to hide her obvious consternation. As the train drew out of King's Cross, I reflected on the ➔

fact that I was the only male amongst seven females - had I struck lucky? Gathering speed, the train made its escape from the dark, drab suburbs of metropolitan London. It wasn't long before Samantha pulled out some lengths of white yarn and a pair of crochet hooks from her bag and began to weave. Having completed a small section of cloth she pulled it apart and repeated the process. Something she did several times during the journey. I couldn't resist asking her why? "Just practising," came her reply.

The four lady companions chatted enthusiastically amongst themselves about their day in London that, like me, had also started in the early hours of the morning in Halifax - probably on the same train. Having struck up the courage to ask the purpose of their trip to London they immediately included me in their conversation. Their objective had been to visit the newly built Olympic Park before taking in other sights of London, but after travelling what back then was then a convoluted route across London, they arrived to find the stadium closed! What do four elderly ladies do in such a situation? They uttered a series of very impolite expletives and made immediate tracks back into the centre of London to take in the other sights. If the tone of their conversation was anything to go by, they had had a great day in spite of not being able to view the Olympic Park.

ABOVE RIGHT | *"I want my time with you" neon sign - St Pancras Station.* ADAM WEST

RIGHT | *Marilyn Monroe looking over the shoulders of Tom Clift - former managing director of Grand Central. Sadly Tom died in October 2012.* PAUL BIGLAND

TOP RIGHT | *A Grand Central train at Halifax station in Yorkshire. True Tyke country.* PAUL BIGLAND

BOTTOM RIGHT | *An incredible story and an amazing chance meeting. Well worth hunting a back copy out.*

There is a certain symbiosis between strangers who engage in chat on a train that cannot be replicated on any other form of transport. My plan to sleep during the journey had been put on the back burner as I joined in with a pleasant and genial round-the-table exchange of opinions about London, travelling on trains and the (then) forthcoming Olympics. I also enjoyed some unexpected treats retrieved from their bags together with coffee from the trolley service. I didn't suspect that the journey would reveal an intriguing insight into the life of Marina, who I had already assumed to be Latino, sitting across the aisle.

Samantha and Mary both alighted at Doncaster, our first stop. From this point onwards the Grand Central train exits the East Coast main line to crawl its way along the back streets of the railway network, via Pontefract, Wakefield, Mirfield, Brighouse, Halifax and finally Bradford.

'WILD CHILD'

As the train pulled out of Doncaster, Marina asked if this was the right train for Bradford. Her accent confirmed immediately her South American origin, and this was quickly picked up by one of the lady companions who assured her that the train did indeed terminate at Bradford. In typically direct Yorkshire fashion, she asked Marina where she was from? "I was born in Colombia, but I am British now", came the reply. "Are you visiting Bradford"? 'No', she answered, "I live there with my husband." At this point it was clear that Marina had suddenly become the focus of attention and the 'lady companions' were setting her up for some serious interrogation. Over the course of the next 40 minutes or so, they extracted an amazing story.

She explained that her name was Marina Chapman and that she was returning from a visit to her daughter, Vanessa, who lived in London. Vanessa was helping her write an autobiography about her life as a 'Wild Child'. My ears pricked up. Wild child sounded intriguing! Marina went on to explain that she was born around 1950 in a

> "National Geographic took her back to the Colombian jungle with a film crew."

Colombian village. When she was around four years old, she was taken from her village and abandoned in the jungle for reasons she has never been able to discover. She then spent several years living amongst families of white-faced capuchin monkeys (sometimes known as 'organ-grinder monkeys') surviving on fruits and nuts.

SOLD!

Marina was discovered by a team of hunters who were surprised to find that she had no language capability. They took her into 'so called' civilisation where she was sold to a brothel in Cúcuta. She learned the basics of language and social intercourse there but unhappy with her predicament, eventually escaped and lived on the streets before being enslaved to a Mafia family. A neighbour called Maruja, realising her plight, rescued her and her daughter, Maria adopted Marina when she was approximately 14. Maria ultimately sent Marina to Bogota to live with one of her daughters who had connections with the city of Bradford via the textile industry. In 1977 Maria sent her children to Bradford and Marina followed in 1983 to become a nanny. It was here that she met her husband to be, John Chapman, a retired bacteriologist and together they raised two daughters.

We were all, to say the least, staggered by her story - although I'm sure we shared a certain element of disbelief. However, her story later became national news when her autobiography 'The Girl with No Name', written by her daughter, was published and later serialised by the Daily Mail. The tale was also picked up by National Geographic who took her back to the Colombian jungle, with a film crew, to test her claims. The verdict was that her story was almost certainly true, and the film was subsequently transmitted on television.

As our train approached Halifax this amazingly entertaining journey sadly came to an end as I, together with the four lady companions, alighted. Collecting my belongings, I bid goodbye to Marina and cast a quick glance back to the far end of the carriage to say a further goodbye to Marilyn Monroe.

Marina's book, The Girl with No Name, was published in 2013 and although it is now out of print, copies can still be found through online retailers or through second-hand resellers such as AbeBooks and World of Books. It is an amazing story.

TRAIN *TRAVELLER JAPAN*

JAPANESE IF YOU PLEASE

THINK FAST AND EFFICIENT TRAINS AND YOU THINK OF JAPAN. **CAROL LONGBOTTOM** VISITED THE LAND OF THE RISING SUN AND MADE TRAIN TRAVEL ONE OF HER HIGHLIGHTS.

Japan has been a world leader in train travel since Tokyo hosted the 1964 Olympics when this technologically advanced nation reinvented itself as a world player in the post-war era.

Although Japan's iconic bullet trains, the Shinkansen, now rank only third in the world for speed, behind the Chinese Maglev and Fuxing Hao; they are still very impressive locomotives with the most recent versions, the H5 and the E5 capable of a top speed of 224 mph. As train travel enthusiasts, Japan had been top of our 'must visit' list for years. So, when my son Michael moved to Hiratsuka, a town south of Tokyo, my husband and I did not wait too long before visiting and to experience the amazing Japanese railways for ourselves. Stephen and I have already enjoyed many of the railways of Europe, including the fast and stylish Italian Frecciarossa trains, the fourth fastest in the world, but we had always felt that Japanese rail was a 'bucket list' thing.

After a tedious ten-hour flight to Beijing, a four hour stop over, and then another four-hour flight to Haneda Airport in Tokyo, we were tired. ➔

LEFT | *The Chureito Pagoda, built in 1963 as a peace memorial, boasts a spectacular view of Mt Fuji. The view is stunning when the sakura trees are in bloom.*
JOMC

TRAIN TRAVELLER JAPAN

THE JAPAN RAIL PASS

The National JR Pass is essential if you want to make the most of this iconic rail system. It needs to be bought in your country of residence before you travel and then activated at a main line station once in Japan.

They are available for periods of seven, 14 and 21 days and at the time of writing a seven-day, standard class adult pass (12 years and older) costs £214 or you can upgrade that to a Green 1st Class ticket for around £70.

Child tickets (six to 11 years) cost £107/£143 for the same duration.

Alternatively, if you are visiting Japan but planning on staying and travelling within a defined region, regional passes are available.

Visit **www.japan-rail-pass.co.uk** for further information.

'ALWAYS ON TIME'

The Japanese tend to obey social rules without rancour, which helps create a calm and orderly atmosphere. This applies to queues too; there are signs marked on the platforms showing where to queue and people abide by the rules. But not everything you hear about Japan is true. For example, it is a myth that all Japanese trains run on time. Even Japanese trains can be delayed by typhoons, flooding and collapsed bridges. However, they are on time so regularly that if there's a delay, commuters can collect a special ticket from the station to present to their boss to explain why they are late to work; a delayed train is the only admissible reason for lateness.

While we were in Japan, we travelled on the normal Japan Rail trains, the Shinkansen, private railways in Hakone and

RIGHT | *Seven Stars Cruise train - observation car.* JOMC

Our first task was to get from Haneda to the little-known Hiratsuka. This was an hour's train journey during Friday night rush hour, with our suitcases. We were not looking forward to it, but it could not have been easier. The staff at the airport information desk were extremely helpful and we were given detailed instructions on how to get to Yokohama and where to change trains for Hiratsuka. Although most travellers, especially outside the tourist hotspots of Tokyo and Kyoto, are Japanese, there is enough English on signs, timetables, maps, and information boards to guide you through the system. We also found that whenever we were unsure of anything, all we had to do was ask and people were unfailingly helpful and polite.

PEPPER THE ROBOT

In Yokohama we even found Pepper, a small robot, able to give us directions. Japan and its railways have a well-earned reputation for politeness, orderliness, and cleanliness. No graffiti on trains or on tunnel entrances; no litter on the platforms or on the tracks and no rude passengers pushing and shoving. It was a pleasure travelling. That is not to say there is not overcrowding. The rush hour trains are so full that white-gloved guards are employed to gently ease commuters into the carriages to allow the doors to close. Once on the train these dowdily dressed salarymen, and some women, read manga on their phones and quietly mind their own business. With 38 million inhabitants, Tokyo is the world's largest city; it can't afford a lot of space for any individual, so the Japanese have had to re-imagine the concept of personal space, hence their invention of the Sony Walkman for example. The commute home is regarded as personal space and it is respected. To help keep the peace, speaking on the phone, as well as eating or drinking are not allowed on the train.

Kamakura, the Tokyo underground and on the monorail. Next time we plan to do even more. For many of these trains we used our JR Rail Passes. However, they are not valid on the private railways, the two fastest Shinkansen – Nozomi and the Mizuho - or the Tokyo underground. For the Tokyo underground you can get a Suica card, which works like an Oyster card.

The JR Rail Pass is not available to Japanese residents, so we purchased our passes before we left the UK. If you choose to do this do not leave it until the last minute as they can take a couple of weeks to arrive. With your confirmation letter you have to go to one of the larger railway stations to activate the JR Rail Pass (not the small town of Hiratsuka) and it can take some time so don't expect to jump on a train within minutes of arrival.

ABOVE LEFT | *Senso-ji temple is also known as Asakusa Kannon Temple. It is Tokyo's oldest Buddhist temple and is one of the most visited spiritual sites in the world.* JOMC

ABOBE | *Shosenkyo, Kofu, Yamanashi Prefecture, Japan. Shosenkyo is where the river narrows, running through the steep gorge between towering, granite crags.* JOMC

"There are private railways operating throughout the country too."

TRAIN *TRAVELLER* | **15**

TRAIN TRAVELLER JAPAN

SHINKANSEN A MUST

Once activated, a JR Rail Pass is great and if used often can save a fortune. Japan's railways are not cheap, but they are good. The Shinkansen is a must for any train enthusiast; people travel halfway round the world to experience this form of travel. It did not disappoint; it was fast, smooth, and with excellent facilities, including the smart, techno Japanese toilets that perform a wide range of functions. The white-gloved guards walked the length of the train throughout the journey and bowed each time they entered and exited a carriage.

Although eating is not allowed on normal trains it is on these intercity bullet trains. We bought bento boxes in Kyoto station for our three-hour journey to Odawara. The bento boxes had several separate compartments, each with a small offering packed with flavour. As with most Japanese meals we had no idea what we were eating but it was very tasty.

"The Shinkansen is a must for any train enthusiast; people travel halfway round the world to experience this form of travel."

The Shinkansen was fast, streamlined, and luxurious but we also delighted in the many different trains on which we travelled. Unlike the bullet trains, with their airplane style small windows, the normal commuter trains have large windows, perfect for sightseeing. As the interior is sparsely populated – around two thirds of Japan is mountainous and heavily forested - many routes follow the coast, giving passengers panoramic views of the ocean. We were also fortunate to see the top of Mount Fuji; we will try to catch all of it next time if it sheds its cloak of cloud. There are private railways operating throughout the country too. You can use your Suica card on some of these, so it is best to check before buying a ticket.

TEMPLES

Kamakura is a delight of a city in the Kanagawa region and boasts three stations together with one of the most famous temples in Japan. Even in the rain it is a gem. The best way to get around is on the Enoshima Electric Train, which weaves its way between the houses. There are dozens of barriers closing off small roads and alleyways as the train proceeds at a leisurely pace from Kamakura to Enoshima, via Hase, where you will find the Great Buddha at the Hasedera Temple.

One of the many surprises and delights of Japanese trains are the windows in the first carriage through which you can see the driver and the track ahead. Once we had discovered this, we made for the front of trains wherever possible, including those on the Enoshima line, normal JR trains, Tokyo underground and the Tokyo monorail, which runs between Haneda Airport and Hamamatsucho Station. We did not need to travel to Hamamatsucho, but the monorail is worth a there-and-back trip. As Tokyo is so densely populated and built-up the monorail offers an excellent space-saving mode of transportation. For a tourist, especially sitting at the front just behind the driver, it offers a ride akin to a rollercoaster as it threads its way between the skyscrapers, above the myriad of criss-crossing roads, above the docks and skirting the busy harbour. And it is covered by the JR Rail Pass, so all this excitement is included.

THEY HAVE GRABBER KITS ON THE PLATFORMS

As Tokyo is so large, the underground system is correspondingly large. It is also busy but if you can navigate the London Underground, you will be fine in Tokyo too. It operates using a similar map and swipe card system.

As previously stated, the Japanese are organised. For example, they have grabber kits on the platforms so that guards; and it must be guards, can reach down onto the →

CLOCKWISE FROM TOP LEFT | *Our Shinkansen arrives.* CAROL L

Shinkansen Bullet Train. JOMC

Interior of Kawasemi Train. JOMC

Seven Stars Cruise Train interior. JOMC

Kawasemi train alongside Kumagawa River. JOMC

Spotless Japanese train. CAROL L

White-gloved Shinkansen guard. CAROL L

TRAIN *TRAVELLER* | 17

TRAIN TRAVELLER JAPAN

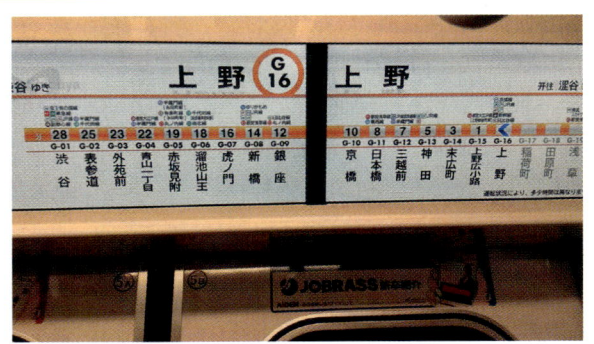

RIGHT | *Information board in Tokyo subway.* CAROL L

FAR RIGHT | *The driver's view on the Enoshima train in Kamakura.* CAROL L

"...train drivers point to each signal as they pass it to help cement passing them in their mind."

ABOVE | *The Kaitoro covered bridge is located in the Shosei-en garden in Kyoto. It has a cypress bark roof and dates to 1884.* JOMC

tracks to retrieve dropped items. This takes a team of three; one to grab the dropped item, the second to keep the crowd back and the third to watch out for trains.

Similarly, train drivers point to each signal as they pass it to help cement passing them in their mind. When you travel at the front of the train you can watch this happen; it is fascinating.

But I think my favourite Japanese rail invention must be the swivel seat. When a train reaches its destination, everyone vacates and then a guard will walk the length of the train turning all the seats to face forwards. As I feel queasy travelling in reverse, I thought this was fantastic.

During our two-week trip to Japan we experienced various aspects of the Japanese railways; and we loved them. Next time, and there will be a next time, the to do list will be much longer and we will travel so much further to see more of this amazing country. We cannot wait.

RAIL ALTERNATIVES

The Shinkansen bullet trains may be Japan's most famous trains but where there is no need for speed there are several other services to savour. Two outstanding examples are the Seven Stars Kyushu Cruise service and the Kawasemi Kyushu Train, both of which are based on Kyushu, Japan's southernmost island.

SEVEN STARS

The Seven Star Kyushu Cruise service, launched in 2013, is an extraordinary deluxe sleeping car excursion train operated by the Kyushu Railway Company. It ranks among the top ten most luxurious trains in the world - matching the Venice -Simplon Orient Express for sheer opulence, luxury, and gourmet extravagance. However, unlike the Orient Express, which consists of original Orient Express carriages meticulously restored, the Seven Star Kyushu Cruise train was built from scratch at a cost of £217m. It comprises seven purpose-built carriages: five sleeping cars, a lounge car, and a dining car, drawn by a specially built, dedicated locomotive.

The train travels through the seven prefectures of Kyushu, an island that boasts outstanding coastal and inland scenery, as well as enjoying a primarily sub-tropical climate, hot springs, and several active volcanoes! For more information visit: www.cruisetrain-sevenstars.jp

THE KINGFISHER TRAINS

Launched in 2017, the cute Kawasemi Yamasemi train was built as a symbol of recovery after the 2016 Kumamato earthquakes. It is a delightful sightseeing train specially created from two standard diesel-powered multiple units.

The two carriages, named Kawasemi and Yamasemi (one painted blue and the other painted green) are named after two species of kingfisher that inhabit the mountains and valleys of Kyushu. The images of these two birds feature prominently throughout the train's livery and interior.

The design for the stylish carriage interiors was inspired by both the birds and the landscape through which the train passes and incorporates cypress and cedar wood taken from the Hitoyoshi/Kuma region, a large part of which was donated free of charge by the local timber industry.

The Kawasemi Yamasemi travels along the Kumagawa River that winds its way through the lush forested landscape between Kumamoto and Hitoyoshi three times a day, a journey time of 1hr 40 minutes. For more information visit: www.jrkyushu.co.jp/english/train

THE DESTINATION FOR RAIL ENTHUSIASTS

Visit us today and discover all our latest releases

- The Modern Railway
- CLASS 56s AND 58s — Mark V. Pike
- THE GLACIER EXPRESS: AN ICONIC RAILWAY JOURNEY THROUGH THE SWISS ALPS — Chris Dyke
- Canals & Railways of Wiltshire — Ken Jones
- CLASS 37s VOLUME 2 — Mark V. Pike
- RAILWAYS AROUND YORK: FOUR DECADES OF CHANGE — Mike Wedgewood
- AC ELECTRICS: CLASSES 91, 92 AND DVTs — Mark V. Pike

FREE P&P* when you order from our online shop...

keybooks.co.uk

Call +44 (0)1780 480404 *(Monday to Friday 9am - 5.30pm GMT)*

*Free 2nd class P&P on all UK & BFPO orders. Overseas charges apply.

TRAIN *TRAVELLER* *UNITED STATES OF AMERICA*

THE CINCINNATI TERMINAL BUILDING

PROPOSALS TO BUILD A UNION STATION IN CINCINNATI WERE FIRST AIRED IN THE 1890S', BUT IT WAS 1931 BEFORE CONSTRUCTION BEGAN AND 1933 BEFORE IT OPENED FOR BUSINESS. **JOHN LEDDSOME** CHRONICLES ITS CHEQUERED HISTORY.

UNION

Cincinnati's Union Terminal building in Ohio is unquestionably one of the finest examples of Art Deco station design in the world. Interestingly, the fact that it got built at all was more the result of conflict than sound planning - taking almost 50 years from first proposals to actual construction. It was also one of the last great Union stations to be built in the US, and the fact that it survives today is more by luck than judgment.

Cincinnati is located in the south western county of Ohio, on the north bank of the Ohio River in Hamilton County. Founded in 1788 it was named after the Society of Cincinnati and honours George Washington who was considered a latter-day Cincinnatus, a Roman called to serve as dictator and who immediately resigned his authority after successfully concluding a crisis. The Ohio River was instrumental in aiding the city's growth and importance, particularly when steam navigation arrived with the construction of a canal creating a water route between Cincinatti and Toledo, Ohio. The railroad arrived in 1836.

In the late 19th and early 20th centuries the city was a staging post for seven rail companies servicing the northeastern, mid western and southern states. However, Cincinnati presented a knotty problem for both passengers and freight traffic. There were five train stations spread across the city (including some in the flood plain of the Ohio River) and only a small percentage of 'through' trains - so it was viewed as a major bottleneck. This state proved to be embarrassing for the local authorities - with one railway publication of the time even cautioning passengers to avoid Cincinnati if at all possible.

REVERED TODAY

Proposals to construct a 'Union Station' - an American term for a station that provides a shared facility for multiple rail services - began in the early 1890s, but it took decades of intense rivalry, frantic discussions, arguments, conflict, lobbying and negotiations - much of which took place during World War One and the nationalisation of the rail network. Even after it was agreed that a central ➔

LEFT | *The spectacular rotunda features the largest semi-dome in the western hemisphere.* CUTM

TRAIN *TRAVELLER* | 21

TRAIN TRAVELLER UNITED STATES OF AMERICA

RIGHT | *A period poster depicting the building and the Pennsylvania Railroad that used to service the city.*
ARCHIVE

MAIN IMAGE | *An impressive night-time exterior shot of the iconic building.*
CUTM

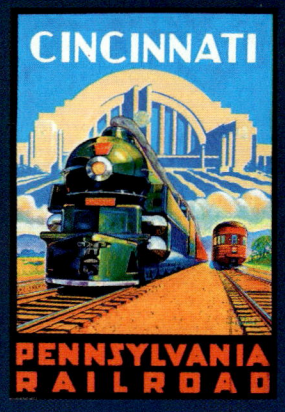

hub station should be built, there were still ongoing arguments about where best to locate it.

Construction finally began in 1931 and the terminal became operational in March 1933. The outcome was not just an outstanding example of Art Deco design but an innovative piece of architecture that is studied and revered by today's designers of modern railway stations - even though its use as a major terminal came to an ignominious end in 1972.

RE-IMAGINED AS ART DECO

The principle architects were Fellheimer and Wagner, a New York practice famed for their railway architecture. Fellheimer was lead designer for the Grand Central terminal in New York, but it was Paul Philippe Cret who was credited with the building's signature Art Deco style. The first outline sketches produced in 1929 were more neoclassical in design - perhaps even Gothic looking. The Cincinnati Union Terminal Company and the Cincinnati Public Works Department were not altogether happy with the look and two years into the construction they amazingly requested that the 500,000 square foot building be re-imagined as Art Deco - reflecting the popular trend of the time!

The magnificent arched frontage is flanked on two sides by towers, each with bas-relief carvings created by Maxfield Keck: the south tower representing Transportation and the north tower representing Commerce. Undoubtedly, the most impressive feature of the building is the rotunda that features the largest semi-dome in the western hemisphere measuring 180ft (55m) wide and 106ft (32m) high. It incorporates two magnificent 22ft (6.6m) high x 110ft (33.5m long) coloured mosaic murals created by Winold Reiss, depicting the history of Cincinnati. He was also responsible for two murals in the baggage lobby, two murals for the arrivals and departure boards, 16 smaller murals (representing local industries) for the train concourse and a large world map located at the rear of the concourse.

Reiss is reputed to have spent two years in the design and creation of these murals. Another artist, Pierre Bourdelle, son of renowned French sculptor Antoine Bourdelle, was also commissioned to design artwork for the terminal, including mosaic murals for the women's lounge, men's lounge, baggage checking area, meeting spaces and the executive offices.

During its brief heyday as a passenger facility it had the capacity to handle 216 trains per day.

HISTORIC **LANDMARK**

Paradoxically, the period in which it was completed coincided with the beginning of a decline in rail travel throughout the USA. By 1939 local newspapers were describing the terminal as a white elephant. After a brief revival during World War Two, use of it declined steadily throughout the 50s and 60s and the creation of Amtrak saw its services reduced to just two trains a day. Amtrak finally abandoned the terminal altogether and Southern Railway acquired some of the land to expand its freight operations.

Fortuitously, the Cincinnati City Council's Urban Development and Planning Committee voted three to one in favour of designating Union Terminal as an historic landmark, thus preventing the entire building from being demolished - although its 450ft (137m) long platforms and concourse did eventually go. The 14 mosaic murals in the concourse depicting key Cincinnati industries were, thankfully, saved and relocated to the Cincinnati and Kentucky International Airport.

During closure the main terminal building was subject to a number of bold attempts to make best use of it. In 1978 it was converted into a shopping mall called 'Land of Oz'. This opened in 1980 with 40 tenants rising to 54 at its peak. However, the recession in 1980 saw a substantial reduction in the number of tenants and despite the Cincinnati Museum of Health, Science and Industry taking space in the building in 1982, the Oz project was forced to close, followed by the closure of a large clothing store in 1985.

Happily, after remaining empty for more than ten years, Hamilton County voters passed a bond levy that saved it from demolition, which led to it being transformed in 1990 into not just the Cincinnati Museum Centre, but as a working station again. Amtrak took advantage of the restoration and introduced 'The Cardinal' - a three times weekly long distance service between New York and Chicago. The entire building has since undergone a series of structural renovations, including the restoration of rooms that formed part of the original building, and this work was completed in 2018.

The Cincinnati Union Terminal stands as a classic example of the period when American railway architecture reflected the romance, scale and importance of the industry. It was bold, exciting and extraordinary and it stands today as a beacon of all that's romantic about rail travel.

> *"Two years into construction they amazingly requested that the 500,000 square foot building be reimagined as Art Deco."*

SUBSCRIBE TODAY!

SUBSCRIBER BENEFITS...

1. **SUBSCRIBER DISCOUNTS** on *Key Publishing* event tickets
2. **SUBSCRIBER DISCOUNTS** on the *Key Publishing* Shop
3. **SAVE** over buying individual issues in the shops
4. **DELIVERED DIRECT** to your door every month
5. **BE THE FIRST** to read the latest features
6. **SIMPLE RENEWALS** with great prices
7. **FREE GIFT** for new subscribers

SIGN UP TODAY!

Sign up to our newsletters to keep up to date with the latest deals

SCAN ME

SUBSCRIBE & SAVE!

PRINT ONLY SUBSCRIPTION
-Annual Direct Debit-

12 issues of *Modern Railways* plus a **FREE gift!**

ONLY £46.99

Please quote: **MR24** when ordering

From the Editor - Philip Sherratt

" *Modern Railways* has been the voice of the rail industry for 60 years, reporting on the latest developments in rolling stock, infrastructure, operations, policy and much more besides.

Each issue of the magazine is packed with the latest news and insightful analysis about developments in our fascinating industry and is the best way to keep in touch with what is going on!

Don't miss out on this great subscription offer! "

SCAN THE QR CODE OPPOSITE TO ORDER DIRECT FROM OUR ONLINE SHOP
shop.keypublishing.com/mrsubs
or call **+44 (0)1780 480404** (Lines open 9.00-5.30, Monday-Friday GMT)

Terms and conditions: Quoted rates are for UK subscriptions only, paying by Annual Direct Debit. Quoted savings based on those rates versus purchasing individual print and digital issues. Standard one-year print subscription prices: UK - £55.99, EU - £71.99, USA - £74.99, ROW - £77.99. *Free gift only available on Annual Direct Debits £46.99 or UK 2 year subscription £99.99, whilst stocks last. Subscription prices and gifts subject to change.
CLOSING DATE: 31st December 2024.

TRAIN TRAVELLER UNITED STATES OF AMERICA

THE CARDI

IF YOU WANT TO EXPERIENCE THE HISTORIC, GRITTIER SIDE OF THE UNITED STATES, COMBINED WITH SOME AWESOME SCENERY, THEN THIS COULD BE THE TRAIN FOR YOU.

More than 190 named passenger train services ran in the USA between the 1890s and 1980s. *The Cardinal* is a descendent of several of them. The Chesapeake and Ohio Railway operated a train called the 'George Washington' that ran between Cincinnati and Washington during the 1930s, with a section from Charlottesville to Newport News. Then, in 1941 the New York Central Railroad introduced the *'James Whitcomb Riley'*, named after the American writer, poet, and best-selling author. This was a daytime train serving Chicago and Cincinnati by way of Indianapolis. Penn Central retained the *'James Whitcomb Riley'* after New York Central merged with the Pennsylvania Railroad. And following the

RIGHT | *Crossing the New River at Hawkes Nest, West Virginia'.*
AMTRAK

NEW YORK

...formation of Amtrak in 1971, the *'James Whitcomb Riley'* went through several permutations, finally being renamed *The Cardinal* in 1977 in honour of the state bird of all six states through which it runs.

AMERICA'S MOST EXCITING CITIES

Operating three days a week throughout the year, *The Cardinal* travels between New York on the Eastern Seaboard to the Windy City of Chicago, located on the shores of Lake Michigan, a distance of 1,147 miles (1,846km). It takes you to some of North America's most exciting cities whilst travelling through the stunning Blue Ridge Mountain chain, the Shenandoah Valley, West Virginia's wild and wonderful white-water rivers, and the 'Great Plains' of North America. These are the highlights.

New York, New York. Famed for its skyscraper landscape, the Statue of Liberty, and its location on the Hudson River, it is one of the world's most restless cultural, financial, and commercial business centres.

Philadelphia, Pennsylvania. Home to the Liberty Bell and Independence Hall where the Declaration of Independence and Constitution were signed. ➔

LEFT | *Passengers boarding the Cardinal.* AMTRAK

LEFT CENTRE | *Statue of Liberty.* NYCGO

TRAIN *TRAVELLER* | 27

TRAIN TRAVELLER UNITED STATES OF AMERICA

TOP LEFT | *The Rotunda at the University of Virginia, designed by Thomas Jefferson.*
MARK LAGOLA AND BEN LUNSFORD

ABOVE | *The view from the rooftop of London House in Chicago.*
CHOOSECH

Baltimore, Maryland. An important seaport and the birthplace of the US national anthem 'The Star-Spangled Banner'.

Washington DC, the country's capital city. Bordering the states of Maryland and Virginia it straddles the Potomac River and is home to the White House, the Capitol, the Supreme Court, and the Pentagon.

Charlottesville, Virginia. Birthplace of Thomas Jefferson and James Monroe, the location of the University of Virginia (a UNESCO World Heritage Site) and a gateway to the Shenandoah National Park located along a section of the Blue Ridge Mountains made famous by both Laurel and Hardy and John Denver's classic *'Take Me Home, Country Roads'*.

Cincinnati, Ohio. Home of the iconic Art Deco Union Terminal building.

Indianapolis, Indiana. Originally home to the Delaware tribe of Native Americans. A major transportation and manufacturing hub nicknamed both the 'Crossroads of America' and 'Railroad City'.

Chicago, Illinois. Located on the windy shores of Lake Michigan, it is one of the largest cities in the USA famed for its bold architecture and a skyline punctuated by skyscrapers - such as the 1,451ft (442m) Willis Tower and the neo-Gothic Tribune Tower.

BREAK YOUR JOURNEY

The Cardinal is a sleeper-service so some of the journey will be overnight and not all the destinations on the route will be visited in daylight hours. However, you can break your journey into segments and spend time in your chosen stop-offs. If you choose to do this, you might not need sleeping car accommodation for every segment. During June, July, and August, you can expect daylight from around 05.30am until around 19.30pm - local times. The schedules are the same year-round so you can easily calculate maximum daylight segments to suit your itinerary. But remember, if you alight at one of your selected stops-offs for a couple of days, then resume the journey to your next destination, whatever time you alight will be the time that you catch the next train for your onward journey - this could be 2am or later!

DRINKS BEFORE DINNER

The Cardinal's sleeping accommodation provides a range of private rooms with amenities for day and night use, from roomettes to bedrooms and accessible bedrooms - some featuring private lavatories and showers.

Passengers who book sleeping car accommodation also enjoy the services of a 'sleeping car attendant' who is responsible for preparing rooms, luggage service and any assistance necessary throughout the journey. They will also take dinner reservations for the dining car and organise drinks before dinner, or you can even arrange for your meal

LEFT CENTRE | *Crossing the Potomac River in Washington DC.*
AMTRAK

LEFT | *Indianapolis Skyline in the fall.*
COURTESY OF VISITINDY.COM

BELOW | *Chicago night view as seen from the Signature Room. A favourite with photographers.*
CHOOSECH

to be served in the privacy and comfort of your room!

Coach seating provides wide reclining seats with leg rests, folding tray tables and overhead lights and you can request at-seat meals and larger pillows for additional sleeping comfort. Sleeping car accommodation charges include meals in the dining car, while coach passengers can purchase dining car meals at reasonable prices. The complete journey takes approximately 26 hours.

For more details go to: www.amtrak.com/cardinal-train

FOOTNOTE

John Denver's 'Take Me Home, Country Roads', was adopted as the official state song for West Virginia. Paradoxically, the Blue Ridge Mountains are in the State of Virginia and only 8% of the Shenandoah River snakes through the state's extreme eastern panhandle. But hey, who cares? It remains one of the most iconic, feel-good songs of the 70s!

"They will also take your dinner reservations for the dining car and even organise drinks before dinner."

TRAIN *TRAVELLER* *GREAT BRITAIN*

SEVEN MILES OF SMILES!

WHATEVER YOUR AGE, WHO CAN DENY THE JOY AND EXHILARATION OF RIDING ON A NARROW GAUGE RAILWAY? ONE SUCH GEM IS 'LA'AL RATTY' – THE LAKE DISTRICT'S AWARD WINNING RAVENGLASS AND ESKDALE RAILWAY. **GRAHAM WEST** MADE AN UNEXPECTED RETURN VISIT.

ABOVE | *The River Mite alongside Barrow Marsh at high tide.*
MARK FIELDING

When some friends asked my wife and I to look after their dog while they took an overseas holiday, we were happy to oblige. We were even happier when, by way of a thank you they presented us with a voucher for a dual visit to Muncaster Castle and a return trip on the *Ravenglass and Eskdale Railway*. This would be a memory lane jaunt for Jen and me as we had visited the 'RER' (not to be confused with the express Paris carrier service) when courting in the mid-60s - we even have the evocative evidence in the form of 8mm cine films in glorious colour!

In fact, I had visited the RER even before then with my parents, when it was still under the ownership of the Keswick Granite Company who ran it as both a passenger and freight line. In those days the carriages were quite basic - most completely open to the elements with uncomfortable wooden bench seats - but that didn't in any way diminish the pleasure (for me) derived from riding behind a real live steam train, chuffing and hissing its way through the then somewhat less wooded landscape and untidier stretches of trackside.

Just seven miles long, the RER is the longest narrow gauge railway in England. It should really be called the railway with 'seven miles of smiles' for this is what you see spread across the faces of its passengers, of all ages, as they ride through this enchanting northwest corner of England, hauled by steam trains bearing uncanny resemblances to characters from *Thomas The Tank Engine*.

NATURE PUTS RIGHT

Our return visit not only revived distant memories of my earliest introduction to this railway, it revealed fresh insights into this relatively quiet part of the Lake District, something my wife and I had both, regrettably, overlooked during our last visit.

RAVENGLASS

BEST EXPERIENCE

Weather permitting, riding in one of the open carriages will give you the best experience. You can listen to the rhythmic, pulsing sounds of the steam engines as they haul their rake of carriages whilst you take in the fresh aromas of the surrounding flora infused with a little steam and smoke from the locomotive!

Take a cushion and a good waterproof jacket if you choose to travel in an open carriage. Although the journey time is around 40 minutes, the weather in this part of the world can change in an instant. Remember also that the journey from Dalegarth to Ravenglass is mostly downhill, so the engine acts more as a brake than a source of pulling power in this direction. The return journey from Ravenglass to Dalegarth is mostly uphill, so this is when you will get to hear the steam locomotives pulling their weight.

LEFT | *RER in the early days at Ravenglass station - former 3ft gauge track still in evidence.* RER MUSEUM

BELOW LEFT | *Reversing into the station.* CUMBRIA TOURISM

MUNCASTER MILL — MITESIDE HALT — MURTHWAITE HALT — IRTON ROAD — THE GREEN — FISHERGROUND HALT — BECKFOOT — DALEGARTH

TRAIN *TRAVELLER* | 31

TRAIN TRAVELLER GREAT BRITAIN

RIGHT | *Northern Rock steaming out of Ravenglass with the stunning estuary in the background.* CHRIS MUNN

RIGHT | *Anyone for a cream tea?* RER

BELOW RIGHT | *Climbing an incline towards Dalegarth.* RER

"The Reverend Wilbert Awdry, creator of 'Thomas The Tank Engine', was a regular visitor."

The concept of carrying tourists on pleasure trips, through often inaccessible but spell-binding landscapes, couldn't have been further from the minds of the company owners who carved out the original numerous narrow gauge railway routes that still exist throughout the UK. Most were built simply to aid the exploitation and transshipment of minerals such as iron ore, lead, slate, coal, clay, and granite to be found in some of the more inaccessible parts of the nation's mountains, hills and hinterland. In their beginnings some had existed as just railway tracks or tramlines utilising gravity as the motive power (in one direction of course) - later gravitating to rope, horse, steam, and diesel power - not necessarily in that order.

Once the mineral deposits became depleted, unworkable, or uneconomic, the lines were mostly closed, and the remaining ravaged landscapes left to the whims of Mother Nature. Thankfully, over time, she came to the rescue, steadfastly masking and restoring much of the ugly remains of the damage caused by this early industrial massacre, by greening and screening with layers of mosses, plants and woodland, providing in the process, myriads of potential sites for fauna of all kinds to hide and build their lairs, nests and shelters. Nevertheless, many of the operators had unwittingly played a pioneering role in the early development of the railway industry, not just in the UK, but throughout the world. They were the first to run a steam locomotive on railway lines, they were the first to carry rail passengers, and they were the first railways to become the subjects of preservation.

WILDLIFE

Known today affectionately as *'La'al Ratty'* (meaning 'little railway' in local Cumbrian dialect) the delightful Ravenglass and Eskdale Railway was the first public narrow gauge railway in England and remains the only one within the borders of Lakeland. Built in 1873 to carry hematite iron ore from the mines at Boot in the Eskdale Valley to the main line at Ravenglass (for shipping onwards to the iron and steelworks of Barrow in Furness) its seven mile route descends almost continuously from Dalegarth station,

some 210 feet above sea level, to the attractive coastal village of Ravenglass, just 17 feet above sea level.

The line weaves its way through the woodlands and fells of the area, with the Scafell range (including England's highest mountain at 3,209ft) clearly visible from the railway just six miles away, and Wastwater, Lakeland's deepest lake (258 feet) just five miles away but hidden from view by the surrounding hills. This is an area where you stand every chance of sighting a variety of native wildlife including buzzards, peregrine falcons, kestrels, curlews, shelducks, greylag geese, ringed plovers, oyster catchers and, if you're very lucky, roe deer, red deer and the very shy red squirrel.

WALKERS, DRIVERS AND RIDERS

There are seven request stops on the line for those who wish to connect to the numerous paths in the area, including one to Scafell Pike from Dalegarth Station (six miles). The RER is also dog friendly so you can take your dog with you if you are planning to walk.

By Road - Access to La'al-Ratty by road is from the A59. Parking charges apply at both stations. The postcode for Ravenglass Station is CA18 1SW while for Dalegarth it is CA19 1TF.

By Rail - The Cumbrian Coast mainline station railway connects with the west coast mainline at Carlisle via Whitehaven - or you can travel from Lancaster (also on the west coast mainline) via Carnforth and Barrow in Furness. The operator for these services is Northern, a British train operating company owned by OLR holdings for the Department of Transport.
For further information, prices and timetables: https://ravenglass-railway.co.uk.

ABOVE | *Scafell Pike, England's highest mountain.* CUMBRIA TOURISM

It comes as no surprise, therefore, to learn that the *La'al Ratty* was a favourite of Arthur Wainwright, one of Lakeland's most famous walkers and writers.

I must include a salient point that was rather forcefully drilled into us by a local who, when approached for directions to a particular lake, commented: "There is only one lake in the Lake District and that is Bassenthwaite Lake - all the rest are meres, tarns or waters!"

In company with many other railway operations of this kind, the line has endured a chequered history, suffering closure and multiple ownerships. Its original inland starting point was the village of Boot, located close to the iron ore mines. When this source became depleted, the line fell into disuse until model makers W J Bassett-Lowke purchased it in 1915 as a test line for their narrow-gauge trains. It was they who converted the line from its original gauge of three feet to its existing 15 inches and by the 1920s had re-routed the line to its current terminus at Dalegarth, just a short distance below the village of Boot. The final climb to Boot was considered too onerous for their locomotives.

In 1946 the Keswick Granite Company purchased the line to haul shipments of crushed granite from their Beckfoot quarry site, but in 1953 this too came to an end and they put the line up for sale. Failing to attract a serious buyer it was sold by auction to the Ravenglass and Eskdale Railway Preservation Society, formed by a mix of locals and railway enthusiasts, with the help of Sir Wavell Wakefield, MP for Marylebone and owner of Ullswater Steamers, together with Colin Gilbert, a Midlands stockbroker who stumped up the remaining cash to complete the purchase. ➔

OPENING HOURS

La'al Ratty runs from March until October. RER also operate special trains during November and December for Christmas through to New Year, including the popular Santa Express and Children's Specials. These must be pre-booked on selected dates. Winter-Warmer trains are run on Boxing Day to New Year's Day on a standard service and February half-term.

There is a cafe at each end of the line, run by the RER. They serve excellent hot and cold meals, sandwiches, drinks, cakes, and biscuits.

TRAIN TRAVELLER GREAT BRITAIN

'River Irt' transported us along a magical mix of long stretches of verdant valley, leafy woodlands, past picturesque stone cottages and along the banks of not one but three rivers in turn - the Rivers Esk, Irt and Mite.

ABOVE | *Northern Rock steaming through the Eskdale Valley with Scafell Pike forming the backdrop.* DAVID MART

INSPIRED BY LA'AL RATTY

Since its formation, the RER has grown into a well organised and efficient operation, acquiring an impressive fleet of motive power in the process. The 'fleet' includes two diesel trains and five steam locomotives - one of which - the *'River Irt'* - is claimed to be the oldest working steam loco of its kind in the world. It was built in 1894 by Sir Arthur Heywood and called originally *'Muriel'*.

The Reverend Wilbert Awdry, creator of *'Thomas The Tank Engine'*, was a regular visitor and was so inspired by 'La'al Ratty' that he based Thomas's chums, *'Rex'*, *'Mike'* and *'Bert'* on three of La'al Ratty's fleet of steam locomotives - the *'River Esk'*, the *'River Irt'* and the *'River Mite'* respectively - hence the similarity! He also based his story *'Arlesday Railway'* on 'La'al Ratty' and *'Jack the New Engine'* - for those who still remember this wonderful series of children's books and television programmes.

Our return revealed numerous changes including the substantial remodelling of their stations and facilities (which is not surprising since our original visit had taken place some 50 years previous!) clearly essential to accommodate the huge increase in the numbers of visitors it now attracts. Happily, none of this development has destroyed the charm this little railway delivers, nor impacted on the journey through the wild, scenic landscape.

It was a bright and sunny day for our most recent visit, and we opted to take our two-way trip from Dalegarth in one of the open carriages - although we did have a choice of enclosed carriages - with or without glass windows. We were just as excited about this trip as we were all those years ago - there is something about this mode of travel that brings out the child in all of us!

The 40 minute, seven mile long journey quickly re-kindled the memories of our original trip as the 'River Irt' transported us along a mix of long stretches of verdant valley, through leafy woodlands, past picturesque stone cottages and along the banks of not one but three rivers in turn - the Rivers Esk, Irt and Mite - their clear waters tumbling and racing their way down towards the estuary, the vista of which provides a stunning conclusion to the termination of the journey at Ravenglass Station. Although we still had the return trip to look forward to, we took some time out to explore not only this interesting little station that rubs shoulders with the Cumbrian Coast main line, but also the village of Ravenglass itself - something we failed to do in the 1960s.

ROMAN HERITAGE

Ravenglass is the only coastal village in the Lake District National Park. It is part of two UNESCO World Heritage sites, a reflection of its Roman history since it was an important naval base for the Roman occupiers around AD130. It was an extension of Hadrian's Wall, the most southerly point of their Cumbrian coastal defence system and the western extremity of the Roman frontier. A garrison of some 500 soldiers was stationed here, and because it was a port, it served as a regional supply centre for other Roman forts in the area, including one located close to the Hardknott Pass - just over three miles beyond Dalegarth - and another at Ambleside, which lies at the head of Windermere. Very little is left of the 300 years of Roman occupation except for the remains of a bathhouse, now called *Walls Castle*, just a ten-minute stroll from the station. It is one of the largest and tallest remaining Roman

AND THERE'S MORE

The RER has recently enlarged its choice of open and saloon carriages, some fitted with heaters and a first-class observation carriage offering large, panoramic windows. There are also two new 'Pullman' class observation carriages called 'Directors Saloon', and 'Ruth' that has dining tables ('cream teas' anyone?) and features balconies at both ends. It can also be set up in different configurations offering flexible seating arrangements and improved accessibilty for wheelchair users.

Increased comfort for passengers will also be available in a new standard carriage with padded bench seating and more headroom.

Another new important introduction is a Changing Places facility for people with complex access needs. Details can found on https://ravenglass-railway.co.uk/plan-your-visit/accessibility.

structures in England, although a good deal of it is missing! Nearby Muncaster Castle, home to the Pennington family since 1208 (and on our itinerary for the following day) is thought to have used stones from a nearby Roman fort in its construction.

Determined to explore Ravenglass village by car we returned in the late afternoon after completing our return trip to Dalegarth on the train. This quaint, atmospheric village looks out across the estuary to the open sea through a distant protective inlet formed by giant sandbanks. With a population of around 250 people the local facilities are, as you would expect, very limited, the village clearly depending on tourism for its survival. The main street runs along the southern edge of the estuary, terminating at a slipway. The sum total of its commercial activities (excluding the RER) appeared to consist of one shop/post office, a dog-friendly hotel and The Inn at Ravenglass (both owned by the Pennington family), a café and a handful of guest houses in the pretty cottages along the street. There is also a great pub called the Ratty Arms. Occupying half of the mainline station, it has a great restaurant that serves reasonably priced food and is where we chose to have our evening meal.

Their dining area features novel railway carriage style booths that run alongside the station platform, separated by glass windows. Whilst sitting in our booth waiting for our meal and mulling over our day, there was an unexpected rumble as a large, ugly mainline diesel locomotive rolled into the station and drew to a halt alongside the Ratty Arms' windows. It was not, as you would expect, hauling half-a-mile of heavy freight wagons, but just four passenger coaches. Its throbbing engine sent pulses of vibration through the station buildings as it waited for just one passenger to disembark. The noise emitted as it pulled away was almost deafening, accompanied by a plume of dense black exhaust!

The sight of this behemoth reduced to such a menial task brought a smile to my face. If this were one of the Reverend Awdry's creations, it would be wearing a look of extreme embarrassment. The stark contrast in scale this locomotive represented compared with those we had experienced during the day on La'al Ratty was palpable!

ABOVE LEFT | *'Joan', the Pullman observation carriage.* RER

ABOVE | *Tides out alongside the pretty village of Ravenglass.* G WEST

BELOW | *Wastwater, Lakelands' deepest lake. Except that it is not a lake apparently, it is just a water.* CUMBRIA TOURISM

BOOK REVIEW

THE SETTLE AND CARLISLE RAILWAY - *PAUL SALVESON* MBE

The history of the Settle to Carlisle railway line must be one of the most publicised railway stories of recent times. The line has been the subject of numerous books, television programmes and even a national TV drama. So, you might ask, what is left to discover that would add anything new to what we already know? The answer lies within this insightful book written by Paul Salveson.

Throughout the book he demonstrates an intimate and eminently meticulous knowledge of the line. From the outset Paul provides a detailed commentary of its route - almost mile by mile - starting not from Settle but Leeds, which is where it once connected with and formed part of the Midland Railway company's high-speed main line route from London to Scotland. His narrative draws attention to other connections the line makes, and once made, to destinations en route, the stunning scenic and rugged landscape it traverses and even the architectural and construction quality of its station buildings that conformed to the Midland Railway's corporate style.

In another chapter he tells the tale of what was considered an 'impossible dream' – a combination of the almost insurmountable terrain the line had to cross and the political hurdles it had to overcome to become a reality – the latter to be re-enacted when its existence was threatened. Whilst he touches on some of the well documented engineering challenges that had to be met to complete this 72 mile (115km) railway - such as the famous Ribblehead viaduct - his book focusses more on the many social consequences that arose during its construction - for many, tragic consequences brought about by poor working and harsh living conditions - exacerbated by the intense driving ambition and force of the company's engineers and management to complete the project.

In a following chapter Paul focusses on the creation of a strong railway community, partly the result of the company building high quality housing for members of its staff who operated the line. Many of these properties still exist but are now mostly privately owned.

It is not until chapter six that you learn why Paul has such an obvious affinity and enthusiasm for the line. In 1966 he took a ride on the train to Ribblehead to take photographs of freight trains from Blea Moor - the tell-tale sign of a true 'railwayac' you might say. Then you discover that in the 1970s he was employed as a guard at the Blackburn depot, with the Settle-Carlisle route becoming one of his regulars. This was the precursor to a career spanning 45 years in roles ranging from guard and signalman to senior management positions for key privatised rail operators. As well as establishing the Association of Community Rail Partnerships (now called Community Rail Network), Paul is currently a visiting professor at the universities of Bolton and Huddersfield, amongst many other key positions he holds on various connected bodies.

Rich Imagery

His book covers many facets of the line's history, including disasters that befell it, locomotives that worked the line and people - past and present - who worked the line, all supported by copious photographs.

By far the most captivating chapter in the book is the one that deals with the constant threat of closure that reared its head between 1963 and 1989. The intrigue, subterfuge and deception undertaken by those that wanted to close it (ever since Beeching's days) countered by the skill, will, passion and resolve by Friends of the Settle and Carlisle Line (FoSCL) who were adamant that it stayed open - makes for a brilliant docudrama. Of course, we know who won.

In the penultimate chapter, Paul recounts how FoSCL, together with the railway companies who operate the line, have since worked in partnership to create the extraordinary renaissance of the line. Cutting its way through the stunning Yorkshire Dales before descending into the verdant Eden Valley, it is not only Britain's highest mainline railway but is recognised as one of the world's great railway journeys.

Paul's book is a tribute to those who conceived it, those who built it, those who died for it, those who worked it and those who saved it.

Although only available in paperback and Kindle versions, the printed version is produced entirely on high quality gloss paper with excellent photo reproduction throughout. **GW**

First published: 2019 by The Crowood Press Ltd
Price: £24
ISBN: 978 1 78500 637 1

TRAIN TRAVELLER *AUSTRALIA*

CAIRNS

DOWN MEMORY LANE

SURPRISINGLY, THERE ARE MORE THAN 70 HERITAGE RAILWAY ORGANISATIONS IN AUSTRALIA. ONE OUTSTANDING EXAMPLE IS THE KURANDA SCENIC RAILWAY BASED IN CAIRNS, NORTHERN QUEENSLAND THAT WAS COMPLETED IN 1891. **KATIE WOODHOUSE** AND HER HUSBAND TOOK A RIDE ON IT.

It was early on Sunday morning and still relatively quiet on the Cairns Esplanade as my husband Mark and I picked our way along what would later in the day become a seething mass of athletic endeavour and achievement; literally hundreds of adrenaline fuelled, tired but motivated individuals competing, mostly against themselves, in a bid to finish one of the most gruelling of multi-discipline races. It was the day of the 2019 Cairns Ironman.

We were heading to Cairns railway station, less than a kilometre from all the action and we had a train to catch and a journey to look forward to - more specifically the Kuranda Scenic Rail journey. With all hire cars booked out and roads blocked off to allow sore legs and mere grams of carbon-fibre and their lycra clad mounts to whizz by as part of the 226 km race, it seemed like the perfect opportunity to finally tick off something that had been on my wish list for almost 20 years.

Back in 2000, I was a lowly Pommie backpacker, exploring and working my way around Australia, and after carefully avoiding the cyclonic wet season, had arrived in the tropical north with a promise of some work at an equestrian centre at a place called Kuranda in the Cairns ➔

LEFT | *Teetering precariously on the Surprise Creek Bridge.*
KURANDA S.R.

KURANDA

TRAIN *TRAVELLER* | 39

TRAIN TRAVELLER AUSTRALIA

FAR RIGHT | *Passengers' view of crossing Surprise Creek Bridge.*
KATIE WOODHOUSE

BELOW RIGHT | *Climbing through the tropical rain forest.*
KURANDA S.R.

hinterland. Alas, the accompanying wage did not amount to much more than a meal ticket and the next bus fare out a few weeks later, but I was there long enough to learn of this iconic railway. The drive to the pretty little village of Kuranda and my place of work afforded views over the magnificent Barron Gorge, with glimpses of railway here and there and of small pods swaying delicately above the rainforest on thin lines of steel which I later learned were part of the equally scenic Skyrail Rainforest Cableway.

WORLD HERITAGE

So here we were, juggling steaming coffee cups, day bags, information brochures and maps, anticipating the arrival of the train that would take us and other small groups of eager travellers up into the glorious World Heritage listed tropical rainforest on a journey into the past. We did not have to wait long. A low deep rumble, palpable through the concrete platform heralded the arrival of the long train; gleaming heritage style carriages towed behind a class 1720 diesel electric locomotive colourfully painted with Buda-dji, the Carpet Snake who, according to Aboriginal Dreamtime, carved out the Barron River and creeks that join it.

Our tickets were for standard class, with our upright, back-to-back, leather bench style seating to be found in one of the burgundy and cream carriages just a few cars from the front. However, before we made ourselves comfortable there, we decided as there was time, to quickly hop onboard one of the more exclusive 'Gold Class' carriages, announced by a shiny brass plaque, and a contrasting livery of dark green and cream, to have a look at what a few more dollars spent would have bought us. Gold class is the KSR premium service, and as you might expect includes attendant service whilst on board, with welcome drinks, morning or afternoon tea and a souvenir gift guide to take away with you once you have managed to prise yourself from the rather comfortable club lounge seats.

POLISHED WOOD, WORN LEATHER

Back in our designated carriage we noted that apart from us there were only a couple more families, so in spite of having designated seats, we were free to roam if desired and sit both in the direction of travel or facing the other way. Sometimes, it is nice to see where you have come from as well as where you are headed.

The smell of polished wood and worn leather was very much in evidence, and alongside framed photographs showing the railway in various stages of construction, the promise of a commentary to accompany our information guides set the stage for a trip back in time and a history lesson. Sadly, the only omission here was a lack of sooty black smoke bellowing from an original steam engine, but needs must, and a lighter, more cost-efficient use of the diesel engine is understandable, if not quite pulling at the strings of nostalgia! A whistle was blown, the engine gave a small but mighty groan and rather like the colourful carpet snake Buda-Dji, we slithered sleepily out of Cairns with 23miles of winding uphill track, tunnels, and bridges ahead. Destination Kuranda, 1,076ft (328m) above sea level.

DENSE RAIN FOREST

Despite it being the middle of winter in Australia, the day was warm and dry. Cairns is in the tropical north of the

"Tropical cyclonic weather, dense rainforest, unmapped territories, lack of infrastructure, let alone the constant threat of being bitten or stung"

40 | TRAIN TRAVELLER

country with generally distinct warm and dry winters and warm and very wet summers - and as we trundled along the first kilometre or two the breeze through the drop-down windows in the carriage was welcome. The sun glinted on the ocean and my thoughts drifted briefly to the men and women already slogging their way around an immensely tough course and how, despite having already been on the go for several hours, they had so many more challenges ahead before they crossed the finishing line. Self-inflicted challenges aside; the challenges faced when this railway was conceived back in 1882 were almost unimaginable by today's standards.

Tropical cyclonic weather, dense rainforest, unmapped territories, lack of infrastructure, let alone the constant threat of being bitten or stung by any number of deadly creatures; these were just a few of the hardships faced by the early pioneers as they boldly set to work, creating new lives for themselves and their loved ones. The catalyst for the creation of a railway took root in Herberton; a ➡

TRAIN TRAVELLER AUSTRALIA

RIGHT | *The train now arriving at Kuranda...*
KURANDA S.R.

BELOW | *Spectacular aerial view of the horseshoe curve and Stoney Creek Bridge as the train makes its way up the steepest part of the journey.*
KURANDA S.R.

small township in the Cairns hinterland where miners were desperate to get supplies after a particularly wet summer brought ceaseless rains and flooding.

In the absence of a navigable route to and from the coast, to ports and cities and towns, the burgeoning success of mining industries as well as those in sugar, tobacco and timber were being thwarted, and the future growth of this part of Australia lay in doubt. The unenviable task of finding a starting point for a railway lay with a pioneering bushman by the name of Christie Palmerston who, working closely alongside the local Aboriginals finally came up with three possibilities. Following months of surveying, the route from Cairns via the Barron Valley Gorge was chosen, shaping the future of this part of North Queensland, and becoming one of the most significant railways in the country.

There were limited 'mod cons' available for use when construction finally got under way in 1886 and although the likes of bulldozers were around, getting these hefty pieces of machinery into dense, often boggy jungle undergrowth was impossible, especially given the exceptionally steep terrain of large sections of the track. For the hardy men employed, it was literally back to basics, dynamite, buckets, spades, and bare hands! Over 2.3 million metres of earthworks had to be cleared to make way for the line, including solid escarpments and embankments.

TUNNELS AND CURVES

Slopes in certain areas averaged 45 degrees with surface debris consisting of loose rock, vegetation, mould, and soil up to seven metres thick.

Travelling sedately in the comfort of a railway carriage and looking contentedly out on the magnificent - and still

dense - surrounds of a World Heritage listed rainforest - the oldest in the world - and hearing these facts and figures, it seemed inconceivable that this had been such a success. However, here we were, trundling ever upwards along a route that incorporated 15 tunnels, 93 curves, and dozens of bridges. One of the most photographed bridges in Australia - Stoney Creek Bridge - spans the wide 80 metre curve and sheer face of Stoney Creek Falls. As it was winter when we were there and therefore the dry season, the falls themselves were at a relative trickle, but at a mere couple of arms lengths away from the carriage windows it was easy to imagine how unnerving it might feel and sound when they are in full flood!

CAREFULLY CRAFTED MECCANO

Mesmerising though the falls were, most pairs of eyes were glued to the view out of the windows on the other side of the carriage. Below us the rock face fell in a sheer knee-wobbling drop, but, as we advanced towards the end of the bridge, we were rewarded with the classic sight of the full length of the train, curving majestically around the bridge, teetering precariously on what looked like carefully crafted Meccano! Possibly the best view of this magnificent rolling stock in action is to be admired (and photographed) as you ascend the infamous Horseshoe Bend. This is the moment you want to be either up near the front of the train or down at the rear end, to appreciate the sight - and sound - of this full-length heavy weight caterpillar being hauled upslope.

Of course, none of these 21st century tourist benefits would have been possible without the dedication and determination of the original planners and bare-handed builders - of which Irish navvies made up a large proportion - in getting the job done. Laying a line in this remote part of the Australian rainforest would be a challenge now, even with civilised accommodation to return to each evening ➡

TRAIN TRAVELLER AUSTRALIA

KURANDA SCENIC RAILWAY
Route: Cairns to Kuranda.
Distance: 23 miles (37km)
Duration: Two hours.
Operators: Queensland Rail Travel.
Web: queenslandrailtravel.com.au

Other trains operated by Queensland Rail Travel
Spirit of Queensland: Cairns to Brisbane - overnight sleeper service and dining room, travels along the lush Queensland coastline. Distance 863 miles (1,390km).

Spirit of the Outback: Brisbane to Longreach. First class sleeper service with communal lounge and diner service. Distance 824 miles (1,325km).

Tilt Train: High speed Brisbane to Rockhampton. Distance 381miles (615km).

The Inlander: Townsville to Mount ISA. Distance 619 miles (997km).

Gulflander: Heritage listed - the Normanton to Croydon line is the only line in Queensland still measured in miles! This isolated railway line is said to go from 'nowhere to nowhere' and to this day retains its patented steel sleepers laid between 1888 and 1891. Distance 562 miles (905km).

RIGHT | *Kuranda Station - one of the oldest in Australia, beautifully decorated with exotic plants.*
KURANDA S.R.

and no doubt a nice cold beer or two as a reward for all that thirsty work. Back in those pioneering days, camps and makeshift accommodation sprang up along the track as it progressed, expanding even into small temporary townships in some places with grocery stores and as many as five hotels at one stage. The incredulity of this is increased when you see the lie of the land from the comfort of your seat now, narrow rock ledges, sheer cliffs, and dense, dense rainforest! I feel sure that workplace health and safety would have something to say about it these days.

TROPICAL GREENERY
And so, onwards to the single 10 minute 'stop' to admire the Barron Gorge dam, before the final leg of this one and a half hour journey, to Kuranda Station, described as "after the style of a Swiss Chalet, the idea being to make Kuranda a show station", which is absolutely spot on! Cloaked in tropical greenery, it is difficult to imagine a prettier place at which to alight after the spectacular journey on the train. Kuranda Station is one of the earliest stations to be built in Australia using standard concrete units and remains the oldest example of its type in Queensland, and these days the beautiful cream coloured buildings themselves are understandably heritage listed.

It is however the planting that takes most credit - and your breath away - for the sheer density and variety of foliage is ingenious, but in contrast to the wild and untamed forests we had just passed through, this tropical backdrop is far more manicured. Taking our cue from the ever vociferous parrots who are always in my experience convinced it is lunchtime, we made our way out of the station (by way of gift shop and tea room), up the steps and over the ornate bridge to the path that would eventually lead us to the village of Kuranda itself. Here we found our own little lunch spot, in a restaurant overlooking the rainforest we had just magically ascended in what now seemed such a short space of time.

Thus 20 years later, having come full circle, here I was again in familiar surroundings; this picturesque village full of artisan shops and curiosities up in the Cairns hinterland, a world away from the chic city we'd left earlier that day. Our return was to be via rail again, but this time SkyRail; a far more modern addition to the landscape but one which once again allowed us to admire, this time from above, the wonderful but harsh landscape which those hardy folk of yore managed to conquer all those years ago.

BOOK REVIEW

SLOW TRAINS TO ISTANBUL — TOM CHESSHYRE

Tom Chesshyre was sitting on a park bench in London with Danny, an old friend, discussing life, when Danny suddenly cleared his throat and asked: "You know Interrail?" He knew very well that Tom 'knew Interrail' as Tom had not only written a travel book called *Slow Trains to Venice* all about the popular European rail passes, but was also a travel hack for various newspapers, having travelled by rail from Peru to Sri Lanka, across the Australian deserts, the Siberian tundra, the Badlands of North Korea, Iran, India, et al. "Tickets are half price right now," Danny continued, "a one-off flash sale to celebrate the 50th anniversary of the company's foundation."

It was this casual mention that was the catalyst for a 4,570-mile adventure on 55 train rides that form the basis of this absorbing travel book. It was not a journey planned by a travel agent. It was to be essentially a 'backpacker's' experience throughout. In one early passage Tom commented that their modus operandi for the trip was "simply to see where the tracks happened to lead on the way to the 'goal' of Istanbul and let serendipity reign and allow whims and fancies to take hold, time-tables permitting."

The only internet connection they agreed to use throughout the trip was the Interrail app on their mobile phones, which proved to be absolutely essential and surprisingly reliable. In essence they wanted to see, hear, smell, touch, and taste what lay ahead. They would witness what they happened to witness, hear what they happened to hear, and meet who they happened to meet, going wherever they pleased whether it was an officially recognised tourist site or not.

So, they both set-off on an Interrail adventure that took them from St. Pancras station in London via Paris, to Strasbourg, Stuttgart, Nuremberg, Passau, Vienna, Bratislava, Budapest, Timisoara, Bucharest, Ruse, Gorna, Oryahovitsa, Sofia, and Svelingrad to end up at Serkeci Terminal in Istanbul.

On reaching Istanbul, Danny was to fly home to re-join his partner, leaving Tom to continue the return leg of the journey by rail (where possible) back to the UK via Kapikule, Svilengrad, Plovdiv, Sofia, Blagoevgrad, Kulata, Thessaloniki, Athens, Patras, Bari, Caserta, Naples, Rome, Balogna, Milan, Tirana, Chur, Visp, Zermatt, Lausanne, Dole, Dijon, Strasbourg, Metz, Luxembourg, Waterloo, Brussels, Ghent, Antwerp, Rotterdam, Hook of Holland, Harwich, and finally London! If you don't know the locations for all of the above, then this book will be a great source of education.

The prime destination was of course Istanbul in Turkey, and it is almost impossible to mention this city in the context of railway journeys without paying homage to arguably the world's most famous train the 'Orient Express' and of course one of its world-famous passengers Agatha Christie. Interestingly, Tom's month-long, unlimited, Interrail travel ticket, covering 33 European countries, worked out at less than 2% of the cost of travelling on the latest incarnation of the Venice Simplon-Orient Express.

Not every journey was by train. For example, one was in the back of a 'BlaBla BMW' car to enable them to get to Passau, their next destination, due to a rail strike in Nuremberg. During Tom's return journey he blagged a lift in a Bulgarian lorry in Kulata, driven by an enthusiastic fruit farmer who spoke remarkably good English, to whisk him through to Thessaloniki to catch a ferry to Athens, there being no train on this stretch.

Throughout the book, Tom delivers interesting and thought-provoking commentary describing the variety of trains they travelled on, people they met, conversations they had, towns and cities they explored, landscapes they passed through, architecture that impressed and depressed them, the variety of food that they ate, dodgy accommodation and locations they stayed in, and how they dealt with a variety of tricky situations. Much of this was of course replicated on Tom's solo return journey.

This enjoyable and illuminating read is a must for both the young and not so young who fancy an Interrailing adventure across Europe. **GW**

(See also 'The Joy of Interrailing - for Oldies', by Carol Longbottom, page 78)

First published: June 2024 by Summersdale
Available as hardback, paperback, and Kindle.
Price: £20 (Hardback)
ISBN: 978 1 8379 9273 7

DON'T MISS OUT ON OTHER KEY TRANSPORT MAGAZINE SPECIALS

If you'd like information about Key Publishing's transport books, magazine specials, subscription offers and the latest product releases sent directly to your inbox. **Scan here »**

TRAIN *TRAVELLER* *GREAT BRITAIN*

THE CALEDON

BRITISH RAIL USED TO USE AN ADVERTISING SLOGAN, 'LET THE TRAIN TAKE THE STRAIN'. IT COULD HAVE BEEN WRITTEN FOR SLEEPER TRAINS. WE LOOK AT THE CALEDONIAN SLEEPER SERVICE — A BUCKET LIST ITEM FOR ANYONE WITH A LOVE OF RAIL JOURNEYS.

IAN SLEEPER

Some might question whether overnight sleeper trains still offer a useful purpose within the UK when, for example, the average journey time between London King's Cross Station and Edinburgh (330 miles) is around four hours 30 minutes; London King's Cross Station to Aberdeen (422 miles) around six hours 45 minutes; and London Paddington to Penzance (253 miles) just over five hours?

The practical answer is they are time-savers. If you're in business and need to travel between both locations, then why waste time and expense by staying overnight at an hotel when you could make the journey overnight whilst sleeping in comfort and arriving at your destination in the morning, refreshed, breakfasted and ready to make an early start?

If you are a tourist the answer is, in all probability, the same. Why stay overnight at an expensive hotel in London, when for a similar price you can sleep overnight whilst travelling to your chosen destination? There is another equally compelling reason, and that is travelling on a sleeper train is quite simply the most romantic, enjoyable, civilised way to travel - bar none. Ask Paul Theroux, one of the most published authorities on rail travel, or retired Church of England priest David Meara, author of a book called *Anglo Scottish Sleepers*, a history of the Anglo Scottish sleeper trains published in 2018. (See book reviews)

The UK's first sleeper carriage was designed and built in 1873 by the Ashbury Carriage Company, a manufacturer of railway carriages based in Openshaw, near Manchester. Its sleeping accommodation was quite basic consisting of stretchers placed between seats - and no bedding. The first recorded use of a sleeper carriage in the UK was also in 1873 when one was attached to a standard train service run by North British Railway between Glasgow and London King's Cross.

LEFT I *The new exterior livery for the Caledonian Express.*

TRAIN *TRAVELLER* *GREAT BRITAIN*

ABOVE | *The Caledonian Express close to the Forth Bridge.* PETER DEVLIN

RIGHT | *The Classic room with single or double bunk beds.*

SURVIVING SLEEPERS

In those days, the average journey time between these two destinations was more than eight hours so an overnight service would have been an attractive proposition for many people. In the same year, Caledonian Railway introduced a London and North Western Railway sleeper service by attaching sleeper carriages to its overnight mail trains on three consecutive days a week, each way between Glasgow Buchanan Street and London Euston. From there on the concept of sleeper services gained momentum at an astonishing pace.

The following year, the Midland Railway Company introduced a sleeper service using Pullman sleeper carriages imported from the US, and in 1877 Great Western Railway launched a sleeper service between London Paddington and Plymouth. The accommodation they offered

was a little more sophisticated than its northern counterparts, having carriages with two dormitories - one with seven gentlemen's berths and the other with four ladies' berths. Another service was added later extending the journey to Penzance, acquiring in the process the rather romantic title of the 'Night Riviera'. Over time, other sleeper destinations within the UK were added, such as Edinburgh, Perth, Aberdeen, Inverness, Stranraer Harbour, Milford Haven and Fort William, plus a Bristol Temple Meads to Glasgow and Edinburgh service. Despite the plethora of bankruptcies, mergers, nationalisation and privatisation that has bedevilled the UK railway industry over time, three sleeper services ➔

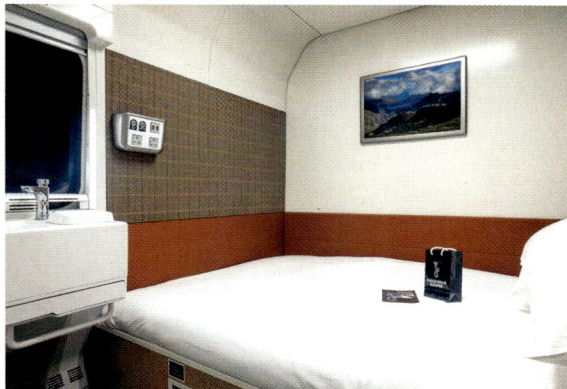

LEFT | *The luxurious Caledonian Double bedroom.*

LEFT | *The Club Car where you can enjoy haggis, neeps, tatties and a range of genuine Scottish whiskies.*

BELOW LEFT | *The Accessible Twin Room.*

'Passengers on the Highlander can enjoy spectacular views from the comfort of their berth as they glide through the heather-scattered moors and mountains of Scotland.'

TRAIN *TRAVELLER* | 49

TRAIN TRAVELLER *GREAT BRITAIN*

ABOVE | *Route map and destinations of the Caledonian Sleeper service.*

have survived - albeit under different ownerships, The Great Western Railway still run the London Paddington to Penzance service, there's the Belmond Royal Scotsman which is more of a tour around the Scottish Highlands than a method of getting from A to B overnight and then there's the Caledonian Sleeper Service. There is also a Eurostar ski service that runs once a week through the winter connecting London St Pancras with French ski resorts but as most of that overnighting takes place in France, for the purposes of this publication it's an overseas service.

In April 2015, Serco, a British owned company providing a multiple range of public services was awarded the standalone franchise for the Caledonian Sleeper service, previously run by First ScotRail.

COMFORT

Over time, Serco introduced a host of improvements offering hotel-style standards of comfort. Caledonian Sleeper rolled out the first of its new fleet of carriages in April 2019 to serve the London to Glasgow and Edinburgh route, called the 'Lowlander'. This was followed in October 2019 by a second fleet of new carriages for the London to Aberdeen, Inverness and Fort William route called the 'Highlander'. The new sleeper carriages incorporate a range of luxury features and four levels of accommodation to meet various budgets.

The base level or standard class offers excellent value airline-style seats designed to allow the base cushion to slide forwards creating an element of reclining without impacting on passengers behind you. There are also personal lockers and charging points. Next step up are the private 'classic' rooms featuring bunk beds, wash basins and access to shared toilet facilities in the carriage. They can be booked for single occupancy and they can also be inter-connected to the adjacent classic room making them a good option for family bookings.

HAGGIS, NEEPS AND TATTIES

The cabins include key-card entry systems, Wi-Fi and air-conditioning throughout. And most importantly, special attention is given to on-board food that features Scottish cuisine, sourced wherever possible from local suppliers including plates of haggis, neeps and tatties, as well a Scotch whisky from a range of distilleries.

When the Highlander arrives at Edinburgh (around 4.30am) it is separated into three sections. One destined for Stirling, Perth, Aviemore and Inverness, another for Dundee and Aberdeen, and another for Fort William.

The Lowlander is separated into two at Carstairs, south of Carlisle - one for Edinburgh and the other for Glasgow. The Glasgow, Edinburgh, Inverness, and Aberdeen portions each consist of up to six sleeping carriages, one lounge carriage and one seats/baggage carriage with bike spaces. The London to Fort William portion consists of just two sleeping-carriages, but you can use the Aberdeen lounge carriage in the evening; another lounge carriage and a seats/baggage carriage is added at Edinburgh for the morning part of the journey to Fort William. Seats only passengers, between London and Fort William, must switch carriages at Edinburgh.

SPECTACULAR VIEWS

The world's best-selling travel guidebook, *Lonely Planet*, has elevated the London to Fort William Caledonian Sleeper service to one of its 'Super Sleeper Trains' making it into its top ten - alongside the Johannesburg to Cape Town and Chicago to San Francisco routes.

Travelling towards Fort William on the West Highland Line, passengers on the Highlander can enjoy spectacular views from the comfort of their berth as they glide through the heather-scattered moors and mountains of Scotland. However, you need to be aware that the best scenic views will be in the early hours of the summer months since it departs from Edinburgh at 04.50am and arrives at Fort Williams just before 10am. Lie in and miss out!

From a leisure traveller's perspective, to get the best out of the Caledonian Sleeper you need to make your way to London to start with and journey north; rolling into the outskirts of London in the early hours of the morning does not, perhaps, represent the most exciting of UK vistas. However, whether you are travelling north or south, business or pleasure, waking up in the morning on a Caledonian Sleeper train, showering and eating a freshly prepared breakfast before alighting is just about as good a travel experience as you can get.

Since June 2023 the Caledonian Sleeper service has been operated by Scottish Rail Holdings, a company wholly owned by the Scottish Government. For more information visit: www:sleeper.scot

LEFT | *Out with the old...* IAN LOTHIAN

BELOW | *...and in with the new.* IAN LOTHIAN

Travelling on a sleeper train is quite simply the most romantic, enjoyable, civilised way to travel - bar none.

TRAIN TRAVELLER **SRI LANKA**

TROUBLED EXOTIC SRI LANKA

THE LUXURIANT, TROPICAL ISLAND WITH ITS PALM-FRINGED BEACHES, LUSH GREEN HILLS AND MISTY MOUNTAINS WAS DESCRIBED BY MARCO POLO AS THE FINEST ISLAND OF ITS SIZE IN THE WORLD. IT ALSO HAS A FINE RAIL NETWORK AS **JOHN HART** DISCOVERED.

RIGHT | *A quite spectacular view from Ella in Sri Lanka's southern hill country.* TIKALANKA

BOTTOM LEFT | *Mihintale, the cradle of Buddhism in Sri Lanka. This statue can be found in the series of five Dambulla cave temples, all of which are open for viewing.* TIKALANKA

BOTTOM RIGHT | *The Sir Thomas Maitland steam locomotive on tour.* VICEROY

As many a stamp collector will attest, Sri Lanka was once known as Ceylon. Surrounded by the Indian Ocean at the foot of the Indian sub-continent, it was a British Crown colony between 1796 and 1948 following earlier occupations by both the Dutch and the Portuguese. It gained independence in 1948 and in 1972 became a fully-fledged republic changing its name to Sri Lanka in the process. Sri means resplendent and Lanka is an ancient name for the island.

It has a rich cultural history with eight World Heritage Sites (the oldest dating back to the 3rd Century BC), and a stunning, diverse environment boasting 86 species of mammals (including elephants and leopards), more than 400 bird species (including 26 endemics), an array of colourful flowering plants and trees, a hill country famous for tea plantations, 14 National Parks, and 995 miles (1,600km) of coastline with palm-fringed, golden tropical beaches.

STUNNING VISTAS

Just 268 miles from top to toe and 139 miles wide, Sri Lanka also has more than 900 miles of railway. Its original railway infrastructure was introduced in 1864 by the British colonial government to transport tea and coffee from the hill country to Colombo, where they had built a port. The local population didn't like the new technology and described them as 'coal-eating, water drinking, sprinting to Colombo metal devils'! Today of course, with one exception, diesel engines power all their trains.

This rail legacy has provided today's tourists with a delightful way to explore the island, with Colombo forming the hub of the network. Access to most parts of the island, north, south, east and west is available by rail from Colombo, with the main line, which heads northeast through the hill and tea country, providing stunning scenic vistas of racing rivers, waterfalls, lush valleys, mountains as well as the spectacle of hundreds of acres of tea estates. Several lines travel along the coastal edges of the island and there are also night trains, but since they pass through some of the island's most beautiful scenery, from a tourist's point of view using them and travelling in darkness would seem rather pointless!

TRAIN TRAVELLER SRI LANKA

The rail network is run by the government and offers first-, second- and third-class travel on the long-distance services, with some first-class carriages providing observation cars. There are also two private companies who run 'specials' by attaching luxury air-conditioned carriages to the regular trains for which they charge a premium price that includes snacks. For those seeking something a little more refined, a privately run steam-hauled luxury tourist train called the 'Viceroy Special' is available on a charter basis and can travel to any destination on the island's rail network. It comes replete with period fittings, a bar, dining and recreation area, plush seating, an observation cabin, on board music, Wi-Fi and four course menus.

Retired firefighter Antoine Julyan visited Sri Lanka last year as a tourist and I asked him about his experiences seeing the island by train.

Kandy to Haputale through the Hill Country

"I'm never quite sure what the difference is between a holiday maker, a tourist and a traveller," said Antoine. "Perhaps an experience-seeker would be a better description - and if it is experience that you are after, then you can do no better than tour Sri Lanka by train. Given their troubled history, the Sri Lankans are remarkably friendly people and ever anxious to impress visitors with their amazing island. They are also very proud of their railway and the staff wear their uniforms with pride.

"You have to be aware that when you turn up at the ticket office to buy your ticket the clerks automatically assume that, because you're a westerner, you will want first class travel with air-con since most Sri Lankan trains offer this option with proper doors and windows - if you can afford it why not? However, you could be denying yourself a wonderful experience. Second class with a seat is more fun, but third class with no seat - perhaps too much fun? Standing crushed against sweaty backpackers for several hours is reminiscent of the London tube and with a similar view - so I suggest this is one experience you might want to forgo.

HOT AND CROWDED

"Most people over the age of 18 would choose a seat and that must be booked in advance. Second class offers wooden seats with some padding, small tables that face the seats, windows that are mostly open and little electric fans that oscillate in a wobbly kind of way. The tables, while very useful for putting food, drink, and maps on, are not recommended for putting your cameras on. They have slippery plastic surfaces that are level with the windowsill and since the trains tilt and rock about quite a lot, you stand a very good chance of waving goodbye to your camera - and it would be a shame to lose all those fabulous pictures you'd just taken!

"Whilst the Kandy to Haputale train is essentially a commuting service for local people and so stops at every station, it carries mostly tourists since it runs through some of the most picturesque parts of the hill country. Although we found this train to be quite hot and crowded on its departure, it did steadily thin out as people alighted at the numerous stops. As it climbed higher into the tea country it not only became cooler but the views across acre upon acre of tea plantations were truly awesome. For these views alone it is worth putting up with anything.

"No commentary on any train journey in any country could be complete without some mention of the toilet facilities! On the Kandy to Haputale train the toilets in the second-class carriage was impressive. By that I mean that the size of the hole in the floor was impressive, clearly designed to reduce any chance of a miss - and the resultant view of the tracks rushing below was quite mesmerising. In a carriage that is constantly rocking to and fro, this is a definite hazard for children and the ultra slim – so beware. On the other hand, it is pure luxury compared to many of the station facilities - and you get a cubicle to yourself!

"In my view, exploring any country is always better by train and this trip delivered some unforgettable experiences. If you do not mind heat, humidity, rocking and clanking and would be happy to endure this for up to five hours, this trip gets my vote."

And the London-based traveller also experienced the southeast coastal line. A very different rail journey to the one through the tea plantations.

GOLDEN BEACHES

Galle to Colombo – Southeast Coastal Line

Away from the tea plantations, the historic city of Galle on the southwest coast is recognised as Sri Lanka's second city. It was hit by a Tsunami in 2004; consequently, much of its architecture has been freshly restored. Amongst its numerous attractions is the magnificent sixteenth century Galle Fort, a UNESCO World Heritage Site. This 200-year-old trading city is steeped in cultural history and has inherited a blend of European colonial styles with Asian influence. Its ancient, meandering streets are lined with bohemian style boutiques, cool cafés, tea merchants picture galleries and stores selling all manner of, →

CLOCKWISE FROM TOP LEFT | *A very traditional dining car in the Viceroy. Note the seating and tables, nothing bolted down here but there's lots of traditional wooden panelling.* VICEROY

A permanent way through the tropical jungle of Sri Lanka. TIKALANKA

Little has changed in 150 years. A typical trackside view in Sri Lanka. TIKALANKA

Waiting for the train at Ella station in the heart of tea country and cloud forests. Ella is 3,415ft above sea level. TIKALANKA

The Viceroy service is a spectacular way to see the high country. VICEROY

An alternative approach to Viceroy dining. 'Modern' rail seating combined with a more restrained use of wooden panelling. VICEROY

"A privately run steam-hauled luxury tourist train called the 'Viceroy Special' is available on a charter basis."

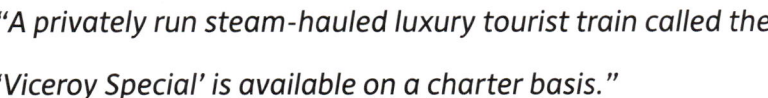

TRAIN TRAVELLER SRI LANKA

handmade artefacts. The city also boasts unrivalled stretches of stunning golden beaches, with mangrove and frangipani trees forming an exotic backdrop.

"Most of the railway journeys across Sri Lanka are truly magical and the Kandy to Haputale service, which traverses the island's lush green hills and mountains, is no exception," continued Antoine. "On the other hand, the train from Galle to Colombo, proved to be a bit of a contradiction as it probably comes closer to an ordinary train journey in parts. As it pulled out of Galle the view was mostly of people's back yards where, in accordance with internationally adopted standards, the trackside was a useful receptacle for general rubbish and junk - just like Neasden in fact!

"Heading out of the city limits we got to see the sort of infrastructure that perhaps we didn't want to see; such as industrial plants and electricity substations, but it did at least provide an insight into the less exotic but essential side of Sri Lankan life. However, once the train made it into the countryside, the stations shrank in size and the level crossings became more frequent.

"It is clear this train forms a vital part of the local black economy. It was fascinating to see local people hop on and off at crossings, maybe for a couple of stops or sometimes they remained on board for the whole journey. Goods and services appeared and disappeared and at regular intervals along the trackside there were small huts whose occupants appeared at their doorways as the train approached to catch small items thrown down to them, most of which seemed to be edible. Once we seated travellers started to open-up our snack-packs, vendors magically appeared in the carriage carrying huge cool-boxes of drinks and baskets of delicious cooked snacks.

TRULY AMAZING

"This was a designated commuter train since there was no choice of accommodation other than second or third class (as always you need to pre-book a second-class seat). The only relief from the heat was air coming through the doors and windows which, when the train was barely moving, was virtually nil. Just over halfway through the journey the crossings and stations started to thin out and the train finally

picked up a little more speed, which was most welcome as the carriage had become almost unbearably hot.

"Interestingly, this route skirts the west coast pretty well most of the way to Colombo, with long stretches of track running right alongside the beach - so close in fact, that spray from the sea could be seen and felt entering the carriage through the open windows. This was truly amazing; we could lean out of the windows and watch the palm trees flick by seemingly inches away and watch families picnicking on the beach just yards from the train. Then in no time at all - or so it seemed, we were approaching the outskirts of Colombo and the sight of its industrial back streets. This journey had taken just over 3½ hours.

"Fort Station in Colombo is the major gateway and terminus for trains into central Sri Lanka; hence it is very, very busy. Built in 1917, the station's design was based on Manchester Victoria station! But that is not the only thing that might be familiar to visitors from the UK. Many of the signal boxes and the old semaphore signals that used to be a common sight on the UK rail network can still be seen still working in Sri Lanka. From a personal point of view, there are two advantages to travelling by train. One is the feeling that you can for a few moments in time, leave reality behind, and two, you get to travel through many parts of a

LEFT | *Stunning is an overused word in travel publications but what other word would suffice? Particularly if you are a tea lover.* TIKALANKA

country denied to others. Sadly, once you arrive at your destination you must leave the train behind and resume normal life."

Martin and Nicole Ashcroft honeymooned in Sri Lanka in 2019. The Cambridge-based couple gave us this account of their 400km rail trip from Jaffna to Colombo.

"Our train journey from Jaffna on the extreme northern tip of Sri Lanka to Colombo started with us braving a tuk tuk ride to the station - we arrived in good time and we were happy to find the train was also set to arrive on time. ➡

ABOVE | *The Temple of the Tooth mirrored in Kandy Lake.* TIKALANKA

LEFT | *Taxi or campervan on rails? Official transport for Sri Lanka railway personnel.* TIKALANKA

TRAIN *TRAVELLER* | 57

TRAIN TRAVELLER SRI LANKA

RAIL OPERATORS: SRI LANKA RAILWAYS

Private Service - The Viceroy Special private train available by charter
North from Colombo: To Jaffna via Anuradhapura and Mannar
South from Colombo: Aluthgama, Hikkaduwa, Galle and Matara
East from Colombo: The Hill Country via Kandy, Nanu Oya (for Nuwara Eliya, Ella to Badulla.
Currency: Rupee - valid only in Sri Lanka
Language: Sinhalese, Tamil, English

UK Tourist Office:
Sri Lanka Tourism, 13 Hyde Park Gardens, Tyburnia, London. W2 2LU Tel: 0207 262 1841

Private UK Tour Organiser: www.tikalanka.com   Map of Sri Lanka courtesy of Tikalanka

We took our spacious reserved seats in first class and the train was clean. Our journey was scheduled to take six hours, so air conditioning was an option we had been unable to turn down. We set off loaded with snacks, books, and drinks, and were looking forward to the possibility of a tea vendor who we imagined would offer the earth's sweetest cups of tea. There was more evidence of a long journey ahead as fellow passengers tucked into Sri Lankan curries for breakfast. They had wrapped them in newspaper and the smell, while unusual first thing in the morning was certainly appetising.

ABOVE RIGHT | *Elephants roam the eastern region.* TIKALANKA

ABOVE RIGHT | *A wide variety of wildlife including the proud leopard.* TIKALANKA

RIGHT | *Palm-fringed tropical beach in Southern Sri Lanka.* TIKALANKA

"The train was very slow, and for most of the journey, extremely bumpy. This gave us the courage to venture out of the carriage only the once; we had not quite found our train legs! This is not a trip for the faint hearted but the experience of one of Sri Lanka's great train rides is something we will never forget - not to say we both would not be sore the next day.

"At one point, the train simply came to a halt. No station, no announcement, the delay apparently caused by a local who had failed to move his cow and cart off the tracks. This was a problem that you'd expect to bring out the worst in people and I can't begin to imagine the reaction were the same to happen back home but here it was met with typical Sri Lankan ease and resolved in good spirit. Travelling in Sri Lanka, you quickly come to realise that time of itself is not important or something to wish for more of but something to appreciate.

"Our windows provided stunning views as the countryside changed from flat, sandy expanses to lush, green fields. And as we headed further south the scenery began to change again from dense jungle to equally dense suburbia; indicating we were getting close to Sri Lanka's largest city.

"We had made significant progress on our books and had tried a few card games. The journey ended up taking about eight and a half hours rather than the scheduled six, but we were not rushing for a flight. We were slightly disappointed that there were no vendors selling tea on the journey. Sri Lankan tea on a Sri Lankan train would have been nice but luckily, we had come prepared.

The sounds and frantic activity of Colombo's station was in stark contrast to the one we had left in Jaffna that morning. We had spent far too little time in that little-known northern city. It had touched us deeply and our thoughts were with the people of the north as they built their lives back from the atrocities of Easter 2019, but we know the residents of Jaffna will do it with that familiar Sri Lankan kindness and welcoming smile."

Sri Lanka has endured more than its fair share of both political instability and environmental destruction in its recent past, as well as sharing the ravages of the Covid-19 pandemic with most of the rest of the world. But none of this has impacted on the undeniable attraction of its stunning landscape, nor the warmth and friendliness of its people. The moment the most recent travel restrictions are lifted we would wholeheartedly recommend that you include it on your list of must-visit destinations.

LEFT CENTRE | *Minneriya and Kaudulla national parks form an elephant corridor for the vast herds that roam the eastern region of Sri Lanka.*
TIKALANKA

LEFT | *The southeast coastal line gets you as close to the sea as it is possible to get without going swimming.*
TIKALANKA

TRAIN TRAVELLER GREAT BRITAIN

RIGHT | *One of the many engine houses seen from the Great Flat Lode Trail. These historic buildings have now been stabilised, which is one of the reasons that this area was designated a World Heritage Site in 2006.* ALL PHOTOGRAPHS TAKEN BY THE AUTHOR UNLESS OTHERWISE STATED

THERE ARE HUNDREDS OF MILES OF DISUSED TRACKS IN THE UK, MANY HAVE BEEN REPURPOSED AS PATHS OR CYCLEWAYS. THE LATE JEFF VINTER EXPLAINED THE HISTORY BEHIND THESE TRAILS.

In 1934, the London, Midland and Scottish Railway closed the scenic narrow-gauge Leek and Manifold Valley Light Railway. The track that linked Waterhouses and Hulme End in rural Staffordshire was then donated to the nation, to be used in perpetuity as a trail. As an example of the rule, 'The grander the company title, the smaller the enterprise', the Leek and Manifold line is hard to beat, but its fate after closure prompts a serious question: was the re-use of its trackbed an isolated incident, or has the same happened to other abandoned railways? Nowadays, about one quarter of the route miles lost to railway closures has been brought back into use as trails, but it was no easy task. Despite the post-Depression 1930s seeing rather a lot of minor railways and bucolic branch lines closing, the example set by the LMS was not followed. It was not followed either in the 1950s, when the British Railways Modernisation Plan offered post-war investment accompanied by further pruning of minor byways, such as Fareham to Alton and Pulborough to Petersfield via Midhurst, both of which puffed into history in February 1955.

The event, which caused a collective national gasp, was the publication of the so-called Beeching Report in March

NOT A TRAIN IN SIGHT

1963, or - to give it its full title - *The Reshaping of British Railways*. Those who used the railways regularly (too few to stave off some kind of economic reckoning) must have examined the report's lists of intended closures, both stations and entire lines, with growing incredulity. In amongst the branches were some seriously major routes, such as Bath Green Park to Bournemouth West, Edinburgh Waverley to Carlisle via Hawick, and London Marylebone to Nottingham Victoria - which, had it been spared, could have served us today as HS2. Its building standards were certainly high enough.

A SUCKER FOR A BARGAIN

Even after the Beeching bombshell, it was nearly a decade before most local authorities began to take much interest in abandoned railways. Two of the trailblazers were at opposite ends of the country: Cheshire County Council opened its 'Wirral Country Park' in October 1973, re-using the old Hooton to West Kirby line after a decade of dereliction, while at roughly the same time Surrey County Council, Hambleton Rural District Council and West Sussex County Council were acquiring connecting lengths of the two railways that once linked Guildford with Shoreham-by-Sea via Christ's Hospital. One can regard West Sussex as a sucker for a bargain. It wanted only a short section of trackbed between Steyning and Bramber, for a new bypass, but staff at the British Rail Property Board were canny: they offered the whole of the line for a price that was too good to resist. The authority snapped up the bargain, dedicated a bridleway over the old railway, and then sold off the land to adjoining landowners. From this unusual start →

BELOW LEFT | *The Treffry Viaduct south of Luxulyan, photographed from just off the lower tramway; the upper tramway runs across the deck. Beneath the deck ran the water supply for waterwheels lower down the valley, behind the photographer.*

BOTTOM LEFT | *The upper tramway in the Luxulyan Valley, with stone sleeper setts still in place, and even some connected lengths of rail.*

TRAIN *TRAVELLER* | 61

TRAIN TRAVELLER GREAT BRITAIN

ABOVE | *The Leek and Manifold line is now a very scenic trail for walkers and cyclists.*
HTTPS://009ADVENTURE.BLOG/

RIGHT | *A railway underbridge on the Tresavean trail near Lanner. This was built by the Hayle Railway, which was opened in stages between 1837 and 1838. For such an early railway, this is a very impressive piece of engineering.*

RIGHT | *Between Wadebridge and Padstow, the Camel Trail features a number of underbridges like this, which many trail users do not see because they pass over on bicycles. Sometimes, it pays to wander off the track and see the engineering beneath one's feet.*

evolved the modern 'Downs Link', which at nearly 37 miles is one of the longest ex-railway trails in the country.

The pace was increasing by 1977, when a local group called Cyclebag was formed in Bristol. This group, spurred into action by Avon County Council's failure to do anything useful for cyclists, took a lease on the old Midland Railway between Bath and Bitton, and converted it into a cycle trail. We now know Cyclebag as Sustrans (the abbreviation stands for 'Sustainable Transport'), and its then fledgling Bath-Bitton route has now been extended to form the immensely popular 'Bristol and Bath Railway Path'.

WHERE DOES THAT GO?

The following year, 1978, saw the formation of a slightly different organisation, Railway Ramblers. Its founder, Nigel Willis, had begun to explore old railways in his spare time, and placed an advert with the *Railway Magazine* to ask if any of its readers would be interested in joining him. While the response was not a flood, it was certainly enough to indicate that Nigel had tapped a national interest, and accordingly he set up a club. But why did his advert light a spark? Nowadays, as one travels around the UK rail network, there are few glaring reminders of just how much that network has been cut back. The evolution of many still operational railways into tree-lined nature reserves, with leaves flapping against carriage windows, has seen to that.

However, in the 1970s, empty trackbeds curved off from almost every major line in the country, and passengers saw these as they passed by. These sightings - and the continuing onslaught of railway closures - kept interest alive, and for some it stimulated a sense of frustration at the sheer waste of it all. Not only were railways being closed, and billions of pounds' worth of infrastructure scrapped, but they were not being re-used in any constructive way, bar a few piecemeal sections of road such as the M4 south of Swindon. The M4 uses a short section of the former direct line from Southampton to Cheltenham – another long-distance closure.

Railway Ramblers is the organisation to look to if you want to get out and explore old railways in these islands. The club is organised into regional groups across the country, each of which arranges its own annual programme. Old railways are not as abundant in the countryside as public footpaths and bridleways, even less so old railways that can be walked or cycled with official blessing; but the club occasionally negotiates access to privately owned old trackbeds, while its members have an encyclopaedic knowledge of old railways of every type and size. For many, this is the real revelation. Apart from standard gauge railways that have 'bitten the bullet', there are also narrow-gauge railways, tramways and plateways. And for the uninitiated, a plateway has L-shaped rails to accommodate wagons with flat as opposed to flanged rims. While this combination will never form a network to equal the UK's public rights of way, there is nonetheless rather a lot of it.

Cornwall is a good place to sample the range of routes on offer, although it is not unique. Wales is another fascinating area, particularly where mountains could be quarried for slate or stone. Dreams of wealth enticed ➔

"Railway Ramblers is the organisation to look to if you want to get out and explore old railways in these islands."

TRAIN TRAVELLER GREAT BRITAIN

ABOVE | Liskeard and Caradon Railway, members of Railway Ramblers are now descending a further incline into Gonamena Quarry, overlooked by several abandoned engine houses. The mast of Caradon Hill transmitting station can just be seen at top of picture. This remote spot was the setting for the final episode of series seven of the popular comedy-drama, 'Doc Martin'.

ABOVE RIGHT | The Leek & Manifold line Tunnel - made safe for walkers and cyclists by internal lighting.
HTTPS://009ADVENTURE.BLOG/

Victorian and even pre-Victorian entrepreneurs to drive tramways into the most unlikely, inaccessible, places. However, let us return to Cornwall. Many visitors will be familiar with the Camel Trail, which re-uses the old Southern Railway's lines west of Bodmin. The main route runs from near the site of the old Bodmin North station to Wadebridge and Padstow, with a branch from intermediate Boscarne Junction (now a station on the preserved Bodmin and Wenford Railway) up to Wenfordbridge.

NO CARRIAGES NOW

If you have never heard of Wenfordbridge, don't worry – neither have millions of others. It is on the southwest corner of Bodmin Moor, near St Breward, and was the site of china clay dries which supplied this ultra-remote railway with freight traffic until 1983. Nowadays, especially during the holiday season, the Camel Trail must rival Sustrans' Bristol-Bath route for popularity, but the views are better - especially west of Wadebridge, thanks to the ever-widening estuary. If you are lucky, you might find the little museum at Wadebridge station open, where you can pause on the platform and recall the question that Sir John Betjeman asked himself: "Can it really be... that this same carriage came from Waterloo?" Alas, no railway carriages call here now, but the hourly buses that travel between Bodmin and Padstow are very useful for anyone exploring the Camel Trail on foot.

Elsewhere in the Duchy, there isn't much more standard gauge railway rambling apart from a short branch line to the southwest of Truro; this starts near Cornwall Council's headquarters and curves around to Newham, not far from the city's Lemon Quay. If ever you walk this line, you will not fail to notice how much more convenient the Newham terminus would be for Truro's modern city centre than the current station, which is some way out to the west, and up a rather steep hill. Unfortunately, passenger convenience was not foremost in the minds of those who closed our railways.

WORLD HERITAGE SITE

So, apart from the Camel Trail and the Newham branch, what other old railways can be walked this far west? The answer is surprising and has much to do with 'The Mineral Tramways Project', which the old Cornwall County Council was working on from the late 1980s. The need for such a project was born initially from the declining state of Cornwall's mining heritage, especially the many distinctive 'engine houses' which accommodated the beam engines that pumped water from the mines below. However, this industry left behind not just its engine houses, but also a considerable mileage of associated tramways. Following their abandonment, some of these had been absorbed into the local right of way network, though not in any coordinated way.

The Mineral Tramways Project has been complete for some years now, and it came as no surprise in 2006 when the Cornwall and West Devon Mining Landscape was designated a World Heritage Site. For the explorer of old

FURTHER INFORMATION

Railway Ramblers: Membership secretary, 27 Sevenoaks Road, Brockley, London, SE4 1RA (£12 p.a. by cheque or PO payable to 'Railway Ramblers') www.railwayramblers.org.uk
The writer, Jeff Vinter sadly passed away in 2023 following a short illness. A highly respected railway historian, Jeff was also chairman of the Railway Ramblers for some time and authored numerous books including *Vinter's Railway Gazetteer* - a definitive guide to Britain's disused railways.

railways and tramways, the west Cornish part of this area offers an extensive network of well-waymarked trails, including much of the early Redruth and Chacewater Railway's network. The 11-mile Coast to Coast Trail runs from Portreath on the north coast to Devoran, west of Truro, on the south coast, re-using the Portreath Tramroad of 1812; and, when that runs out, it links into the eastern arm of the Redruth and Chacewater. The Tresavean Trail and Portreath Branchline Trail are much shorter, but the former has wonderful cross valley views as it skirts Lanner, while the former includes the historically important Portreath Incline.

It may feel strange to climb a hill when following an old railway, but that is what railway inclines did. Some used stationary steam engines to provide the power, while others were 'self-acting', with loaded wagons going down providing the power to raise empty wagons going up, all connected via a continuous loop of extremely strong cable. The one route in the tramways network that, at first glance, does not appear to be based on old rails at all is the Great Flat Lode Trail, which forms a 7½-mile circuit of Carn Brea. This is the route on which to see Cornish engine houses, for there are vistas here that take in a dozen of them at once. If you have time and the inclination, look up the local large scale OS maps on the National Library of Scotland's website: choose the earliest ones, generally from the 1870s, and you will discover that much of the Great Flat Lode Trail is rail-based after all, mainly due to its incorporating short lines that connected various mines with their associated 'stamps', or stamp houses, where the ore was broken up for mineral extraction. Some of these stamp houses are the size of cathedrals.

ROYAL TRAIN

Away from the Mineral Tramways, there is still more. The 3½-mile Pentewan Railway, which once linked St Austell with the tiny port of Pentewan, still does, but now as a multi-use trail, although little railway/tramway atmosphere remains. However, that is made up for by the walking in the Luxulyan Valley, north of Par. From near Par station, one can follow the old Par Canal up to Ponts Mill (where the Royal Train used to be parked when in Cornwall) before exploring the remains of some of Joseph Treffry's tramways. Two of these run up the valley, one below the other. The upper route is the more impressive, for it includes many 19th century rails and sleepers, still in situ.

By contrast, the lower route passes a massive set of china clay dries. Approaching Luxulyan, one reaches Treffry's Viaduct - actually a viaduct and aqueduct combined - that gives the lie to the notion that tramways do not feature large engineering works. If all that doesn't impress you, then you can head east across the River Tamar and try out the network of 'Tamar Trails' between Tavistock and Gunnislake. Some of these originate from the Devon Great Consols Railway, a product of the area's copper boom in the 1840s. During the warmer months, these West Country places may now be restful getaways, but within the last two centuries they have been very, very different. Exploring them will cast a fascinatingly different light on the area, and there are enough suggestions here to fill a week comfortably.

LEFT | *An ever-growing number of former trackways are finding new life and new purpose.*
MATT JESSOP

BELOW | *The Bissoe coast to coast cycle trail and mineral tramway.*
MATT JESSOP

TRAIN *TRAVELLER* CANADA

IN 1885, CANADIAN RAILROAD ENGINEERS FINALLY COMPLETED THE RAILWAY THAT LINKED WESTERN CANADA WITH EASTERN CANADA, CREATING IN THE PROCESS THE DOMINION OF CANADA. **GRAHAM** AND **JENNY** BOOKED A TRIP ON THE ROCKY MOUNTAINEER'S FIRST PASSAGE TO THE WEST TRIP THAT FOLLOWS THE ROUTE FROM VANCOUVER TO BANFF.

VANCOUVER

THE ROCKY MOUNTAINEER

It was dark when we clambered into a taxi to take the short journey from our hotel in downtown Vancouver to the Rocky Mountaineer's western terminus. We were anxious not to miss our 0640am check-in. Having flown into Vancouver five days earlier, we had spent the time we had there exploring this beautiful city. Despite a superabundance of high-rise buildings, Vancouver has retained a satisfying human scale in its development. Its location silhouetted against a backdrop of tiers of hills and mountains, a sparkling waterfront and a profusion of wide tree-lined streets make the city an appealing place. The weather had been glorious throughout our stay, which only enhanced the lure of this vibrant, cosmopolitan, British Columbian metropolis.

It was still dark when we arrived at the station, an austere building with a minimalist facade, but since it had originally been constructed in 1945 as a locomotive repair shed for the Canadian National Railway, you can forgive its lack of architectural merit. It was transformed by Rocky Mountaineer Rail Tours and opened as their station in 2005. However, from the moment we entered the building, any pretence to austerity was diminished in an instant for we received the friendliest and warmest of welcomes - an attitude afforded to everyone as they arrived. If anyone knows how to make their guests welcome, the Rocky Mountaineer crew do. Everything delivered with typical, laid back Canadian politeness.

The Rocky Mountaineer is not a sleeper, so the trip is divided into two days with an overnight stay in the town of Kamloops. Of course, this meant that we would enjoy the scenic splendour of the entire 560-plus mile (900km) journey during daylight. Having checked in our luggage, the next time we were to be reacquainted with it would be in our hotel bedroom! We had chosen to end our journey at Lake Louise, just 36 miles short of the Banff terminus to spend a couple of days exploring before finishing the trip by road. ➔

LEFT | *Travelling through the Rocky Mountains.*
COURTESY RM

HOPE — SPUZZUM — LYTTON — ASHCROFT — SAVONA — KAMLOOPS — CRAIGELLACHIE — REVELSTOKE — LAKE LOUISE — BANFF

TRAIN *TRAVELLER* | 67

TRAIN TRAVELLER CANADA

ABOVE | The Rocky Mountaineer skirts its way around the edges of Sefton Lake on the Goldrush Route.
COURTESY RM

RIGHT | Departure time at the Rocky Mountaineer station.
VAN-CC

BELOW RIGHT | Vancouver's trendy waterfront marinas.
G WEST

Whilst waiting for departure we were served with drinks and snacks and entertained by a highly accomplished pianist playing a magnificent grand piano; his repertoire embracing everything from Gershwin to Rachmaninov and Scott Joplin to Andrew Lloyd Webber - all performed with aplomb, despite competing with a steadily mounting crescendo of voices as the building filled with more excited passengers.

FULL HIGHLAND REGALIA

A glance around confirmed that the dress code was, thankfully, no dress code. There was not a cocktail dress, bow tie, tuxedo, or dinner suit to be seen - just an egalitarian mix of T-shirts, skirts, jeans, cargo trousers, chinos, cagoules, and trainers. When the time for departure arrived, a staff member called everyone to attention and to make the occasion more of an occasion, a kilted piper dressed in Highland regalia appeared and piped everyone out of the building and onto the waiting train. This was not going to be a Paul Theroux-style train trip!

The train consisted of a rake of 16 carriages, more than half of which were huge double-deckers designated for passengers who had booked 'Gold Leaf' service. The remaining single-decker carriages were for passengers who had booked economy 'Silver Leaf' service. We had booked 'Silver Leaf' so were not expecting to be pampered quite as well as our double-deck neighbours. However, our carriage had two wonderful hosts, a young self-conscious culinary team member and its own galley. Jen and I settled down into our remarkably comfortable, reclining seats arranged airline fashion, providing oodles of leg room and drop-down tables large enough to accommodate a full canteen of cutlery, crockery, drinks, and cameras. Large panoramic windows and wrap-over skylights ran the length of the carriage providing clear, unobstructed views to the horizon.

A pleasant aroma of freshly brewed coffee permeated its way through the carriage from the direction of the galley as our hosts welcomed everyone on board with a toast and explained the programme, protocols and expectations for

the first half of the trip. With every seat in the carriage occupied there was a palpable air of excitement as we eased away from the station.

Two powerful diesel-electric locomotives in matching livery haul the train; power not speed is the essence of this journey since the locomotives are required to haul this lengthy train to a height of 5,338 feet (1,627m) as it traverses the Rocky Mountains. Making its way out of the Vancouver suburbs the train crosses British Columbia's longest river, the Fraser, at a point just over a mile short of the end of its 850mile (1,370km) long journey between the northern Rockies and the Pacific Ocean. The train then curves around to join the line that follows the Fraser's northeastern bank for some 160 miles (258km) where, at the village of Lytton, the Fraser is joined by the Thomson River. We would then track the Thomson River for another 95 miles (153km) until we reached Kamloops in the early evening, where we were to stay overnight.

Since it was an early morning start, we were served with breakfast from airline style trolleys soon after we set off. The breakfast menu included freshly baked Cinnamon scones, three-cheese omelettes served with peppered chicken, sausages, skillet potatoes and roasted tomatoes, rounded off with a field berry parfait - all skilfully prepared and served on pristine white crockery, together with a choice of fruit juices, coffee or tea. This, perhaps, is where Gold Leaf service departs from Silver Leaf. In Gold Leaf you travel upstairs to enjoy the sights and move downstairs to prepared tables for your meals. I cannot offer any comparisons between the two standards, but the food served in Silver Leaf was delicious and plentiful. Having both slimmed in preparation for our holiday, it quickly became clear that our five day stay in Vancouver, plus our two days on board the Rocky Mountaineer, was going to rapidly restore the status quo!

After travelling southeast of Vancouver for some 38 miles (61km) along the flood plains of the Fraser, we arrived at the small town of Mission. Here the line divides into two (or converges depending on your direction of travel) with both lines continuing to run parallel with each other but on opposite sides of the river - all the way through to the village of Lytton 126 miles (202km) away. Located within a thickly wooded area it was no surprise to discover that this area was home to the Mission Municipal Forest - which also explains why Mission was once noted for being the world's largest supplier of red cedar shakes and shingles. ➔

LEFT | *'This is where we are folks!'*. G WEST

BELOW LEFT | *The deep blue water of the glacier-fed Lake Louise.* G WEST

"If anyone knows how to wow people, the Rocky Mountaineer crew do."

ONE AND A HALF MILES IN LENGTH

The Rocky Mountaineer took to the northern side of the river as it curved east heading towards the southern foothills of the Garibaldi Mountains, and then crossed over the Harrison River at a point where it merged with the Fraser River. This river drains Harrison Lake, which at 38 miles (61km) in length and almost 5.5 miles (9km) across is the largest lake in the southern Coast Mountains of Canada.

The landscape thus far had been relatively low lying and dominated primarily by lush green forestry, however, as we neared the town of Hope, the trees began to thin out and we could see the shapes and forms of the southern edges of the Lillooet range of mountains to our north. Here the river ran wide and fast, its deep turquoise water now providing the only land-based contrast to the beige coloured, rocky embankments that began to dominate the landscape. For me this journey was proving to be a geographical education since I was sadly ignorant of the

RIGHT | *Lunch Time on the Rocky Mountaineer.* G WEST

ABOVE | *The old telegraph posts alongside the Thomson River are a reminder of times past.* G WEST

fact that the Canadian Rocky Mountains were not located immediately behind Vancouver as I had imagined, but almost 300 miles (482km) inland, separated by several other mountain ranges as well as the great Thomson and Fraser plateaus!

The 'first passage to the west' was completed in 1885 having broken through the Rocky Mountains via the Kicking Horse pass. This was followed in the early 1900s by a second route via the Yellowhead Pass, located farther north near Jasper. These two routes converge near Kamloops but on opposite sides of the Thomson River and were used by competing Canadian railroad companies of the time - Canadian Pacific Railways (CPR) and Canadian National Railways (CNR). Today both lines are shared by three railroad operators; the Rocky Mountaineer (a privately run tourist company), VIA Rail (the national passenger carrier that uses the Yellowhead Pass for its 'Canadian' Vancouver to Toronto TransCanada service) and CN (the national freight carrier). These two lines interconnect with each other across the Fraser river in several places allowing the trains to swop sides - depending on the density of traffic, their intended destinations or to avoid any obstructions that may occur.

Common in the United States and Canada, freight has priority over passenger traffic, so passenger-carrying services are subject to frequent stops to allow freight traffic to proceed. This is not that surprising when you see the length and size of their freight trains. Many are hauled by up to four locomotives and often exceed one and a half miles in length with some bearing full sized 40ft containers mounted in double-decker format, so starting and stopping these leviathans must call for an enormous amount of power and skill.

At the rear of our carriage, beyond the exit door was an open deck area that provided an unrestricted, windowless vantage point on either side from which we could take photographs. This was a wonderful facility for those wanting unrestricted shots of the scenery - the only problem was, when approaching an area that promised a special photogenic opportunity, there was a mad dash to the deck resulting in a bit of jostling to gain an advantageous spot. The folks in the double-deck carriages also had balconies on their lower decks but they were a little larger so there was more of an opportunity to find an unoccupied vantage point. We could take pictures through the large panoramic windows although as these were tinted the results were invariably impaired.

MOUTH WATERING

Approaching the town of Hope, where the line swings north to head between the eastern edges of the Lillooet Range and the western edges of the Cascade Mountains, we passed through the first of many tunnels cut into the jagged rock-side, the double-deckers dodging the roof by inches - or so it seemed. Originally a First Nations settlement, the town of Hope was founded in 1808 by explorer Simon Hope. In 1848 the Hudson Bay Company built a trading post here called Fort Hope and in 1858 the Fraser Canyon Gold Rush contributed further to its growth. Hope officially became Canadian along with British Columbia in 1871. Today the town is classified as a commuter town although, with a population of just over 6,000 people, it is difficult to understand just where the commuters commute to or from since the town is quite remote and more than 80 miles from Vancouver.

Occasionally, we could see one of the long freight trains casually snaking its way along on the other side of the river and, periodically, we would slow to a halt to allow a freight train to pass on our side of the valley. All the while the crew ambled up and down the aisle dispensing refreshments and of course lunch, as well as providing interesting and informative commentary on the areas we were travelling through. The lunch menu was mouth-watering and included sliced tomato salad, a choice of grilled salmon cooked in a creamy dill sauce, or short ribs braised in Okanagan Valley Merlot with creamy garlic mashed potatoes and roasted root vegetables - accompanied by a choice of red or white wine, fruit juice and followed by a choice of dessert and coffee. What better life experience can there be than sitting on a slow-moving train journeying through some of the most spectacular scenery on earth while being served with food and drink by attentive hosts?

Thus far we had seen little wildlife other than a few bald eagles, some nesting cranes, and strange looking sheep. Assurances were given that although moose, deer, black bears and elk roamed the areas we were travelling through, we would be more likely to see them and the occasional grizzly as we delved deeper into the Rocky Mountains the following day. However, the drivers provided a novel wildlife lookout service by notifying our hosts of anything of interest for them to bring to our attention.

BEYOND HOPE

One interesting trackside feature were the remains of telegraph poles installed soon after the railway was completed to provide a communication network, not just for the rail companies, but also a telecommunications link between eastern and western Canada. No longer in use, they stand, or mostly lean drunkenly, still linked in places ➔

ABOVE | *Hell's Gate where the river, compressed between rock faces just 111ft (34 metres) apart, becomes a maelstrom as 750 million litres of water forces its way through the gap every minute - more than the entire volume of Niagara Falls.* G WEST

BELOW | *A freight train on the opposite bank of the Fraser near Cisco Crossing. The freight drivers enjoy fantastic views from their office windows!* G WEST

by drooping cables attached to ceramic insulators mounted on the crossbeams. Frustratingly, trees growing alongside the track occasionally blanked out views of the valley and beyond, which is when 'Gold Leafers', sitting higher up in the double-deckers might have gained an advantage over those of us in the single-deckers below - but it's a minor gripe.

There is of course, a very good reason the railway followed the river courses for they had carved a path through this wild and unforgiving terrain over millions of years. Every so often though, the line would break away from the river and climb up onto the valley-side to avoid what one would assume to be an unnavigable stretch. These diversions delivered some amazing views and hair raising moments when the track was laid perilously close to the edge of a high embankment and when the train slowed

RIGHT | *Top deck on a Rocky Mountaineer double decker.* COURTESY RM

BOTTOM RIGHT | *Trackside in the Fraser River Valley.* G WEST

> "The train slowed to almost walking pace to cross precarious looking bridges that spanned the numerous ravines."

to almost walking pace to cross precarious looking bridges that spanned the ravines, chasms, creeks and waterfalls that cleaved their way down the hillsides.

Although we were travelling through large tracts of wilderness, from time to time we passed small neighbourhoods occupied by First Nations people. One such settlement 30miles (51km) north of Hope was located along a narrow strip of land between the railway line and the river. It was known collectively as Spuzzum Indian Reserve No. 1, Spuzzum Indian Reserve No. 1A and Spuzzum Indian Reserve No. 7. Humorously referred to as 'Beyond Hope', Spuzzum was the subject of a song in the early 1980s by a band called "Six Cylinder" with the refrain "If you haven't been to Spuzzum, you ain't been anywhere". These neighbourhoods served as a reminder that the indigenous First Nations people would have travelled this route in their canoes and on horseback for thousands of years before the unwelcome arrival of foreign people in covered wagons, stage-coaches, trains and latterly, the Trans-Canada highway.

A few miles beyond Spuzzum we arrived at a point known as Hells' Gate where the river, compressed between a formidable sheer gorge with walls just 111ft (34 metres) apart, becomes a maelstrom as 750 million litres of water forces its way through the gap every minute - more than the entire volume of Niagara Falls.

You should never judge a place on face value and travelling past what appeared to be a tiny, insignificant settlement called Lytton, with a population of just 250 people, proved the point when we were to discover later that it had played a pivotal role in the formation of British Columbia. Founded during the Fraser Canyon gold rush in 1858-59, Lytton sat on the confluence of the Fraser and Thomson Rivers, an area that had been inhabited by the Nlaka'pamux First Nations people for more than 10,000 years. Paradoxically, it was also one of the earliest locations settled by non-natives in the southern interior of British Columbia.

CAKES, BERRIES & NUTS

Originally called Fort Dallas by non-natives, Lytton was named after the English novelist Bulwer-Lytton who had served as governor of the then colony. An entry in Wikipedia reveals: "When news of the Fraser Canyon Gold Rush reached London, Bulwer-Lytton, who was Secretary of State for the Colonies, requested that the War Office recommend a field officer, "a man of good judgement possessing a knowledge of mankind", to lead a Corps of 150 (later increased to 172) Royal Engineers, who had been selected for their "superior discipline and intelligence". The War Office chose Richard Clement Moody and Lord Lytton. Moody was charged to establish British order and transform the newly established Colony of British Columbia into the British Empire's "bulwark in the farthest west" and "found a second England on the shores of the Pacific." Lytton desired to send to the colony "representatives of the best of British culture, not just a police force": he sought men who possessed "courtesy, high breeding and urbane knowledge of the world," and decided to send Moody, whom the Government considered to be the archetypal "English gentleman and British Officer."

Lytton was also a friend and contemporary of Charles Dickens and one of the pioneers of the historical novel 'The last Days of Pompeii'. Even today he is held to account by literary aficionados for penning what they consider to be one of the worst opening sentences in the English language - the opening line to the novel Paul Clifford: 'It was a dark and stormy night'! However, Bulwer-Lytton is also responsible for the well-known metonymy 'The Pen is mightier than the sword'. Today, the village of Lytton is occupied primarily by First Nations people whose name for the place is Camchin - also spelled Kumsheen meaning "river meeting".

Lytton is also where we crossed over the Fraser to join the northern bank of the Thomson that courses its way between the southern end of the huge Fraser Plateau and the northern tip of the Okanagan-Thomson Plateau. The plateau is a high, dry belt interior grassland and forested area that harbours rattlesnakes, ground creeping prickly pear cactus, sage bush, and tumbleweed. As we gently threaded our way along the edges of the Thomson River, which in places was so wide it had the appearance of a lake, we were served afternoon tea that included fresh cut sandwiches, cakes, berries and nuts - the very epitome of civilisation!

The final part of the day's journey took us past two other rail-side communities. One, called Ashcroft, named after Ashcroft Manor, located nearby which was founded by two English brothers, Clement and Henry Cornwall. The brothers emigrated to Canada from Gloucestershire in search of gold, but on hearing stories from failed prospectors decided to establish a place to give future hopefuls somewhere to buy provisions and saddle their horses.

Approaching the southern tip of the beautiful Kamloops Lake we passed Savona - another former gold country community named after Francois Savona who, in 1859 established a ferry service across the Thompson River. The first steamboat ever built in the interior of British Columbia, the Martin, was launched in Savona. Sadly, the era of the steamship came to an end when the Canadian Pacific Railroad reached Savona from Port Moody in 1885.

Crossing a long, low bridge over the Thomson at the far end of the lake we finally rolled into the City of Kamloops where once again the impressive, slick Rocky Mountaineer organisation revealed itself. Lined up at the station was a fleet of coaches - one for each carriage, waiting to carry us to our hotels. Our luggage, transported by road from Vancouver, had arrived ahead of us and already been deposited in our rooms. Such luxury.

It was to be a 6.15am start the following day so we had little chance to explore Kamloops (population 90,000) other than to meet up with two relatives who had travelled up from Vernon (a mere 54 miles away) to enjoy a meal out in a noisy but delightful local restaurant. Breakfast was again going to be served on board the train, so all we had to do in the morning was get up, wash, dress, pack our cases and head down to the foyer in time to board our transfer coach.

KAMLOOPS TO **LAKE LOUISE**

Back on board, the aroma of coffee and breakfast being prepared once again wafted through the carriage - a welcome prequel to what proved to be a very different second half of our journey. The previous day had been gloriously sunny, but clouds had formed overnight and as we rolled out of Kamloops, they completely masked the upper reaches and peaks of the mountains. The terrain between Kamloops and Lake Louise is far more rugged than the area we'd travelled through on the previous day, as we were now entering an area dominated by mountains to the north, east and south - if only we could have seen them! Rocky Mountaineer run another trip called 'Journey Through the Clouds' that travels between Vancouver and Jasper. This also overnights at Kamloops, but then heads north alongside the North Thomson River, whereas we were heading east along the South Thomson River. For a moment, we thought we were on the wrong train! ➡

TRAIN TRAVELLER CANADA

THE ROCKY MOUNTAINEER
1100-980 Howe Street. Vancouver, British Columbia, Canada. V6Z 0C8. Telephone: 604.606.7200.

Rocky Mountaineer operates train journeys over three principal routes:
First passage to the West which travels along Kicking Horse River, terminating in Banff. Rocky Mountaineer is now the only passenger rail service that operates on this route. **Journey through the clouds** travels through the coastal mountain range and the Fraser Canyon following the route of the Fraser River, then the North Thompson, terminating in Jasper. And **Rainforest to Gold Rush** is a three-day trip that begins in North Vancouver, with stops in Whistler and Quesnel. This route terminates in Jasper.

GoldLeaf
Operating on all routes, Rocky Mountaineer's GoldLeaf service uses a custom- designed, bi-level, glass-domed coach with full-length windows and reclining seats that can be rotated to accommodate groups of four guests. Guests are offered hot meals prepared on board the train, served to them in the lower level dining car. Beverages and snacks are also available throughout the journey. The two levels of the GoldLeaf coach are accessible by a spiral staircase or an ADA elevator.

SilverLeaf
Operating on the same routes as GoldLeaf, Rocky Mountaineer's SilverLeaf service uses a custom-designed, single level glass domed coach with oversized windows and reclining seats. Guests onboard are attended to by two to three onboard hosts and offered a hot entrée option for breakfast and lunch served at their seat and plated to their preference. Complimentary beverages are served throughout the journey, including wine, beer, spirits, and non-alcoholic drinks. Gourmet snacks are also offered throughout the journey.

The nearest international airports to Rocky Mountaineer are the Calgary International Airport and Vancouver International Airport. In Vancouver, Rocky Mountaineer trains depart from the Rocky Mountaineer Station, while other rail services operate out of either Pacific Central Station (Amtrak and Via Rail) or Waterfront Station (West Coast Express). At the Jasper railway station passengers can transfer directly to Via Rail's Canadian (Vancouver to Toronto service) and Jasper (Prince Rupert service).

In the UK, Rocky Mountaineer tours can be booked through a variety of independent travel specialists.

Little Shuswap Lake, which at an elevation of 1,138ft (346m), forms the head of the South Thomson River, was partially hidden by mists floating just above the surface and drifting up into the hillside - creating an entrancing, mystical feel. The name Shuswap, or Secwepemc is derived from another tribe of First Nations people. Little Shuswap Lake forms on the western extremity of the much larger Shuswap Lake, shaped like the letter H it extends to more than 50 miles. The Rocky Mountaineer followed a twisting route around the southern edges of the lake before arriving at a place called Craigellachie (definitely not a First Nations name) where it slowed to a crawl alongside a memorial commemorating the ceremonial driving of the last spike into the rail-ties that completed the CPR's 'first passage west' route in 1885. We then proceeded to climb up to Eagle Pass that cuts through the Monashee Mountain range at an elevation of 1,804ft (550m), roll past the Clanwilliam Lake (1,739ft - 530m) before descending into Revelstoke, a small city founded in the 1880s. Although it has a population of just over 6,000 people, in Canada it seems that any community with a population of more than 100 can be called a city! Originally called Farwell, after a local landowner and surveyor, it was later changed to Revelstoke by the CPR in appreciation of Lord Revelstoke. He was the head of Baring Brothers & Co., the UK investment bank who, in partnership with another UK bank Glynn Mills & Co. saved the CPR from bankruptcy in the summer of 1885 by buying the company's unsold bonds, enabling the railway to reach completion. Revelstoke is located close by Revelstoke Mountain, at 6,500ft (1,981m) rated as one of the finest ski resorts in the world.

KICKED BY HIS HORSE
Leaving Revelstoke the tracks parallel the Illecillewaet River and from here on in the two diesel locomotives really start to earn their keep by forging their way along twisting river gorges and climbing to the summit of the Rogers Pass (4,364ft -1,330km) near Glacier National Park. The route then cuts across the Selkirk Mountains and descends into the Rocky Mountain Trench - also known as the Valley of a Thousand Peaks. This is a very long wide valley (up to 16 miles wide in places) that sits at an average elevation of between 2,000 and 3,000ft and extends all the way between British Columbia's border with the Yukon in the north, to Montana in the US. We travelled south along the eastern edges of the Rocky Mountain Trench until, just beyond a small town called Golden, the line meets the Kicking Horse River and proceeds to follow it through the Kicking Horse Pass that forges its way through the Rocky Mountains towards Lake Louise and Banff. At 5,339 feet (1,627m) the Kicking Horse Pass was the key to the route that made the 'first passage west' possible - it is also the highest point on the journey.

First explored in 1858 by the British North American Exploring Expedition known as the Palliser Expedition, Kicking Horse Pass is not, as is often surmised, an indigenous tribal name, but a name acquired after James Hector, a naturalist and geologist on the expedition was kicked by his horse while exploring the region. The original CPR route through the pass was known as 'The Big Hill', and with a gradient of 1 in 23 (4.5%) was the steepest stretch of mainline railroad in North America. When built it was a temporary solution since the gradient was twice the limit normally allowed for a downhill track. The very first construction train to go down the pass ran off the hill and landed in the Kicking Horse River, killing three people. Despite introducing a maximum speed limit of just 8mph, together with several safety features designed to reduce the possibility of an accident, accidents continued to happen. Bedevilled by these and the need to use expensive 'pusher engines', the CPR eventually diverted the route and built a pair of spiral tunnels through the mountain, each one just under 1,000 yards in length. Although adding several miles to the route the tunnels reduced the gradient to a more manageable 1 in 46 (2.2%).

GRIZZLY BEAR

As we edged along the twisting path of the river that raced and churned its way through the narrow confines of the Kicking Horse Pass ravine, a slight change in note from the two locomotives in the form of a 'thrum' was all we were aware of as they turned on the power to make the ascent. Entering each one of the pitch-black spiral tunnels we could sense their curvature as a mild form of centrifugal force, but other than that, ensconced as we were in the luxury of our carriages and having been waited on royally since leaving Kamloops, we were unaware of the height we had attained. As we emerged from the second tunnel, a brief break in the clouds revealed glimpses of snow-capped mountains for the first time on our journey - but there was still no sign of any local wildlife! To be fair, the dark interiors of the forest that lined the track on both sides could have hidden any number of creatures - in fact they could have been standing just feet away from the train and we wouldn't have seen them! As we neared Lake Louise, there was an excited shout from one of the hosts who pointed in the direction of the trees suggesting that there was the outline of a grizzly bear in there. It was indistinct, stationery and could just as well have been a cardboard cut-out! The fact that we failed to see a single moose, deer, black bear, or elk did not detract in any way from the enjoyment of the journey. Our onboard hosts had contributed in no small measure with their friendly, willing, and courteous manner of keeping us well-nourished with wonderful food and drink - as well as keeping us entertained with humorous and informative commentary about the areas we passed through.

As the train drew to a halt at Lake Louise station, we gathered our belongings and very reluctantly proceeded to alight. A coach was waiting close by to take us to our hotel, which was less than a mile away, with our luggage already stowed in its hold. The beautiful log cabin style building that serves as Lake Louise's station featured in the 1965 epic drama *Dr Zhivago*. It provided a fitting end to our journey and as we dined in our hotel that evening, snow began to fall adding a magical finale to the day.

By morning, the snow had disappeared, and we ventured out to view the lake that was just a few hundred yards away. Although the sun had appeared the lake was hidden by a curtain of mist. Happily, the mist soon evaporated to reveal a spectacular, snow-covered backdrop, perfectly mirrored in the deep-blue surface of the lake. Sitting at an elevation of 5,740ft (1,750m) Lake Louise was named after the fourth daughter of Queen Victoria who was the wife of the Marquis of Lorne, Governor General of Canada from 1878 to 1883.

There are not enough superlatives in the dictionary to adequately describe the scenic grandeur we had witnessed during our two-day journey on the Rocky Mountaineer. It really was the trip of a lifetime. Can we do it all again please?

BELOW | *Curving through the Rockies near Banff.*
COURTESY RM

"There are not enough superlatives in the dictionary to adequately describe the scenic grandeur we had witnessed..."

SUBSCRIBE TODAY AND SAVE £££s!

TOP TEN BENEFITS OF SUBSCRIBING...

1. **NEW BENEFIT -** *Hornby Magazine* subscribers can **SAVE £20** on **Railway Touring Company main line steam trip tickets!** Visit **www.keymodelworld.com/railwaytouringcompany** for more information.
2. **DELIVERED DIRECT** to your door every month
3. **SAVE** over buying individual issues in the shops
4. **SUBSCRIBER DISCOUNTS** on the *Key Publishing* Shop
5. **NEW EXCLUSIVE MONTHLY OFFERS** direct to your inbox
6. **SUBSCRIBER DISCOUNTS** on *Key Publishing* event tickets
7. **BE THE FIRST** to read the latest features
8. **PRIORITY ACCESS** for new Key Model World Shop products
9. **FREE GIFT** for new subscribers
10. **SIMPLE RENEWALS** with great prices

SIGN UP TODAY!

Sign up to our newsletters to keep up to date with the latest deals

SCAN ME

SUBSCRIBE & SAVE!

HORNBY magazine

WRITTEN BY MODELLERS FOR MODELLERS

PRINT ONLY SUBSCRIPTION
- 1 year (UK) -

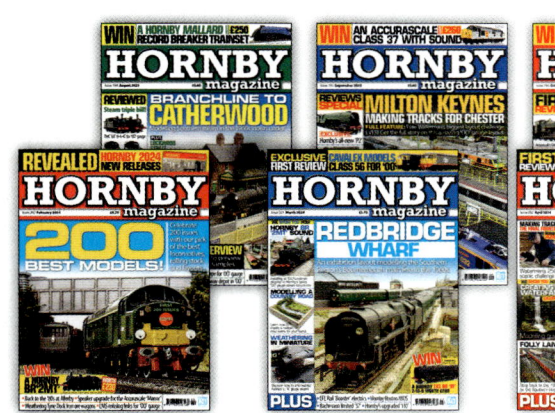

12 issues of *Hornby magazine* plus a **FREE gift!**

ONLY £55.99

Please quote: **HM24** when ordering

From the Publisher - Mike Wild

"Here at Hornby Magazine we are all at the heart of the hobby and in every issue we bring you the latest model railway news, product reviews and features you won't find anywhere else.

Each issue of the magazine is packed full of inspirational modelling articles from our dedicated team to give you all the information you need to build your own model railway or inform you about your next purchase.

Don't miss out on this great subscription offer, and our new discount ticket offering with the Railway Touring Company."

SCAN THE QR CODE OPPOSITE TO ORDER DIRECT FROM OUR ONLINE SHOP

shop.keymodelworld.com/hmsubs

or call **+44 (0)1780 480404** (Lines open 9.00-5.30, Monday-Friday GMT)

Terms and conditions: Quoted rates are for UK subscriptions only, paying by one year print. Quoted savings based on those rates versus purchasing individual print magazines. Standard one-year print subscriptions: UK - £55.99, EU - £69.99, USA - £72.99, ROW - £75.99. *Free gifts only available to UK customers and only on one year print subscriptions, whilst stock lasts. Gift subject to change. *This is a limited time offer and subject to availability whilst stocks last. *Saving based on the total cost of 12 issues and BR Diesel Brake Tender B964040E Plain BR Green worth £36.99. Total subscription savings £50. **CLOSING DATE:** 31st December, 2024

TRAIN *TRAVELLER* **EUROPE**

THE JOY OF
INTERRAILING -
FOR OLDIES!

THERE IS A REAL SENSE OF ADVENTURE WHEN EMBARKING ON A LONG TRAIN JOURNEY; AND THE JOY OF INTERRAILING IS NOT JUST FOR THE GAP-YEAR GENERATION. **CAROL LONGBOTTOM** REPORTS THAT EVEN THE MATURE TRAVELLER CAN ENJOY THE MANY ADVANTAGES OF TRAIN TRAVEL, ESPECIALLY IN EUROPE.

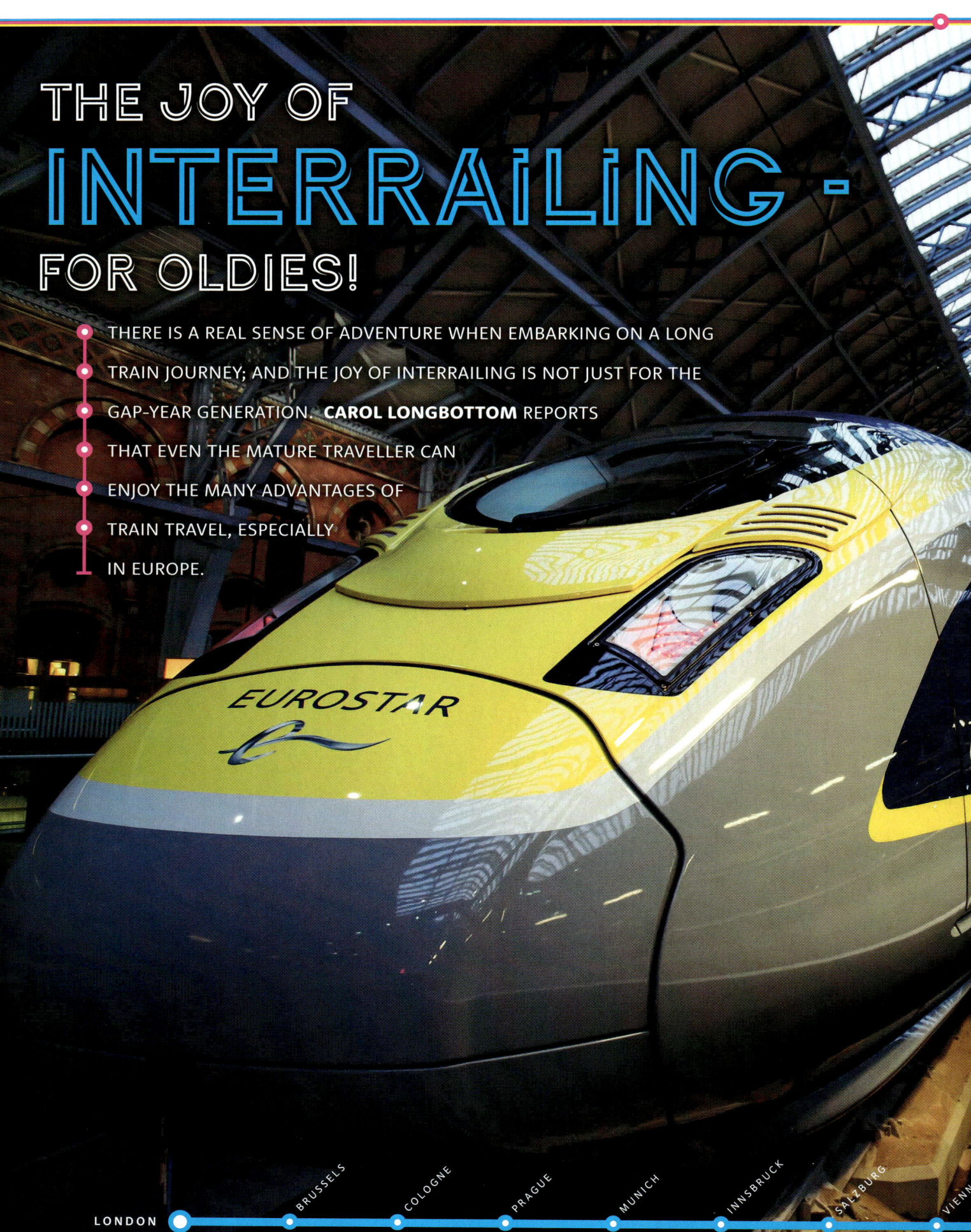

LONDON — BRUSSELS — COLOGNE — PRAGUE — MUNICH — INNSBRUCK — SALZBURG — VIENNA

The United States and Canada may have the stunning open vistas and Japan and China the speed, but European train travel can boast diversity, of people, places, and perspectives. And the trains are great too. My husband and I recently enjoyed three weeks of European Interrailing visiting 15 cities in seven countries to celebrate a significant birthday; and it was not my 21st!

Travelling over 3,000 miles we definitely let the train take the strain; sitting back with a beer, musing over our guidebooks, and making friends with our fellow passengers. No need to organise airport transfers; train stations are situated at the heart of any city and anticipation builds as each one reveals itself during the final leg of the journey. Between each destination the countryside rolls by with ever-changing and often dramatic scenery, from the grandeur of the Alps to the almost magical crossing of the Venetian lagoon.

Although the romantic notion of turning up at a station with little idea of the next move may appeal to some, we decided that detailed planning was required to enable us to make the most of our extended holiday. Knowing exactly where we were going, on which train and at what time, and even which seat, made life so much easier, and possibly a lot cheaper too as in the early planning stages we'd decided against a rail card because many of the services we wished to use were excluded. ➔

LEFT | *Eurostar Train at St Pancras Station.* ITR

TRAIN TRAVELLER *EUROPE*

"We were impressed with the top speed of the Salzburg-bound train, at 220kph, approximately 140mph, until we experienced the smooth 300kph (186mph) on the Italian Frecciarossa."

ABOVE | *The Italian Frecciarossa High Speed Train.* HITACHI

ABOVE RIGHT | *Prague Castle.* VISIT PRAGUE

BELOW | *Cologne Cathedral across the Rhine.* ITR

FANTASTIC HOSTELS

We also booked all our accommodation months in advance, giving us the best selection, which proved invaluable as many hostels only had one or two double or en suite rooms available. Hostels can be fantastic; like train stations they are often situated in the city centre and so offer affordable and comfortable lodgings without the need for taxis or public transport. Designed to welcome visitors from all over the world, many travelling alone, hostels are friendly and lively. You are always made to feel welcome, sometimes with free beers and always with a city map. We were, without exception the oldest guests in every hostel we visited. No problem, we are young at heart.

London was our first port of call where to my amazement and delight I discovered Thomas Crapper toilets in the ladies in the Parcel Yard pub at King's Cross Station. We took Eurostar to Brussels, for a quick turn-around to catch a comfortable and fast train to the charming city of Cologne. One night and one day here before we caught the cosy overnight sleeper to Prague.

An invaluable resource for planning any train journey, The Man in Seat 61 (www.seat61.com), recommended setting the alarm for 7am to enjoy the beautiful scenery; he was right, as always. We meandered along wide green valleys whilst eating our breakfast, delivered direct to our cabin by the train's porter.

Prague was gorgeous. We could not find a single ugly building, in the centre at least. Our hostel was just off the Charles Bridge, a perfect location, and offered half price Segway city tours. Having never experienced Segway

travel before it was amazing how quickly we mastered the art. We were hooked; these machines are great fun but come with a hefty price tag. Arriving mid-morning in Prague we had just 24 hours in the city. As with Cologne we will have to revisit.

DELIGHTFUL SALZBURG

The train to Munich was slow and pleasantly old-fashioned. We shared our six-seater compartment with an elderly lady returning to her home in Munich and a young Australian of Chinese descent taking time out from his medical training to explore Europe. We shared picnics and stories in German and English; the six-hour journey was a pleasure, as was Munich with its BMW World, Olympic Park and bierkellers. From Munich it was on to Innsbruck, just for an afternoon, before onto Salzburg. The mountain view from Innsbruck station is stunning and well worth the detour.

For many years, the French TGV trains have been the envy of British commuters, but I can vouch for the German, Austrian and Italian trains too. The train to Salzburg had large comfortable seats, plenty of room and lots of information displayed on monitors in each carriage. We were impressed with the top speed of the Salzburg-bound train, at 220kph, approximately 140mph, until we experienced the smooth 300kph (186mph) of the Italian Frecciarossa. Incidentally, Eurostar also tops 300kph but does not shout about it.

Salzburg was delightful. Tea on the veranda of Schloss Munchstein, a five-star hotel and spa overlooking the town, is recommended, so too is a visit to the Augustinian

ABOVE LEFT | *Marienplatz - Munich.* A. MUELLER

ABOVE | *BMW World. Well worth a visit if you are interrailing through Munich.* A. MUELLER

BELOW | *Beautiful Salzburg.* CAROL L

RIGHT | *Schönbrunn Palace Gardens, Vienna.* ITR

BELOW | *Gorgeous Venice.* CAROL L

Brewery; a hidden gem for good beer and food frequented by the locals. Our next destination, Vienna, is also worth a second look.

With our packed itinerary we dipped our toes into each city; quickly packing our bags again; we saw this trip as a taster menu. The first course was Germanic in flavour, visiting Belgium, briefly; Germany, twice; the Czech Republic and Austria; the second course was Italian, with stops in Venice, Florence, Naples, Sorrento, Rome, and Turin. The trip from Vienna to Venice can be made on the sleeper but we opted to see the Alps, not sleep through them. The train was packed and not for the first time we were thankful for our small rucksack each as we watched tiny Asian girls drag huge, coffin-sized suitcases from carriage to carriage looking for safe storage.

TO TURIN

Venice is spectacular and arriving by train is magical, not only the bridge across the lagoon but also stepping out of

LEFT | *The beautiful mountains and valleys of Austria.* ITR

BELOW | *Grand Canal Railway Station - Venice.* CAROL L

"*Venice is spectacular and arriving by train is magical, not only the bridge across the lagoon but also stepping out of the station straight onto the Grand Canal.*"

the station straight onto the Grand Canal. Even for seasoned travellers it is a delight, as is Venice itself. Although it can be an expensive tourist trap there are opportunities to experience Venice without breaking the bank. The Vaporetto, waterbuses, provide an excellent and affordable transport system and it is a joy just to wander aimlessly along the alleyways that criss-cross the canals.

Florence was a flying visit, of just less than 24 hours, and then down to Naples, which charmed and horrified in equal measure. Naples is very busy, smelly, and lively. Seeing a family of four balanced precariously on a speeding scooter is nothing out of the ordinary and there is graffiti everywhere, especially on the stations and high-rise apartment blocks that crowd the rickety Circumversuvius train that connects Herculaneum, Pompeii and Sorrento. We enjoyed both ➔

Naples and Sorrento, but they are not high on our 'must visit again' list. Our enforced stay in Naples station due to train delays and subsequent seat confusion because of over allocation threw a negative shadow over our visit. However, it was the only blip in our entire trip; every other train was punctual and well organised.

Rome was wonderful but our delay meant a curtailed stay; another city to revisit later. Our train to Turin was one of the rail highlights of the holiday; a Frecciarossa 1000. We had booked Premium Standard, with leather seats and complimentary drinks and snacks and were entertained by two very animated businessmen travelling to Milan. Like Cologne, Turin was a delightful surprise, beautiful mountain-framed setting, with ornate buildings and grand piazzas. After a delicious meal we stumbled across a public dancing session in the main square with dozens of people jiving; we joined in, but the style was much slower than the jive we dance at home.

We had decided to finish our journey with a flourish and went First Class on the TGV to Paris. However, in comparison to some of the trains we had enjoyed around Europe the TGV left a lot to be desired. It was dirty and tired and inadequately staffed. There was no Wi-Fi on the train, and no complimentary drinks, snacks, newspapers or even magazines in First Class and we missed the information. Unlike the Italian trains we had no information on speed, the weather at our destination not even a map showing our present location; all disappointingly low-tech. We had a short stay in Paris and then home again through the Tunnel.

Homeward bound our three-week adventure was over; it had flown by and despite our very busy itinerary the train journeys between each destination gave us breathing space. We found having only a short time, often just 24 hours in a city, helped focus the mind and so we refused to feel guilty about not visiting all the top 'must-do' tourist hot spots; instead we enjoyed exploring; allowing each city to reveal itself to us. Europe is a beautiful and fascinating continent and travelling by train the perfect way to see and experience it.

BELOW | *Sunbathing Platforms - Sorrento.*
CAROL L

BOOK REVIEW

AROUND THE WORLD IN 80 TRAINS - *MONISHA RAJESH*

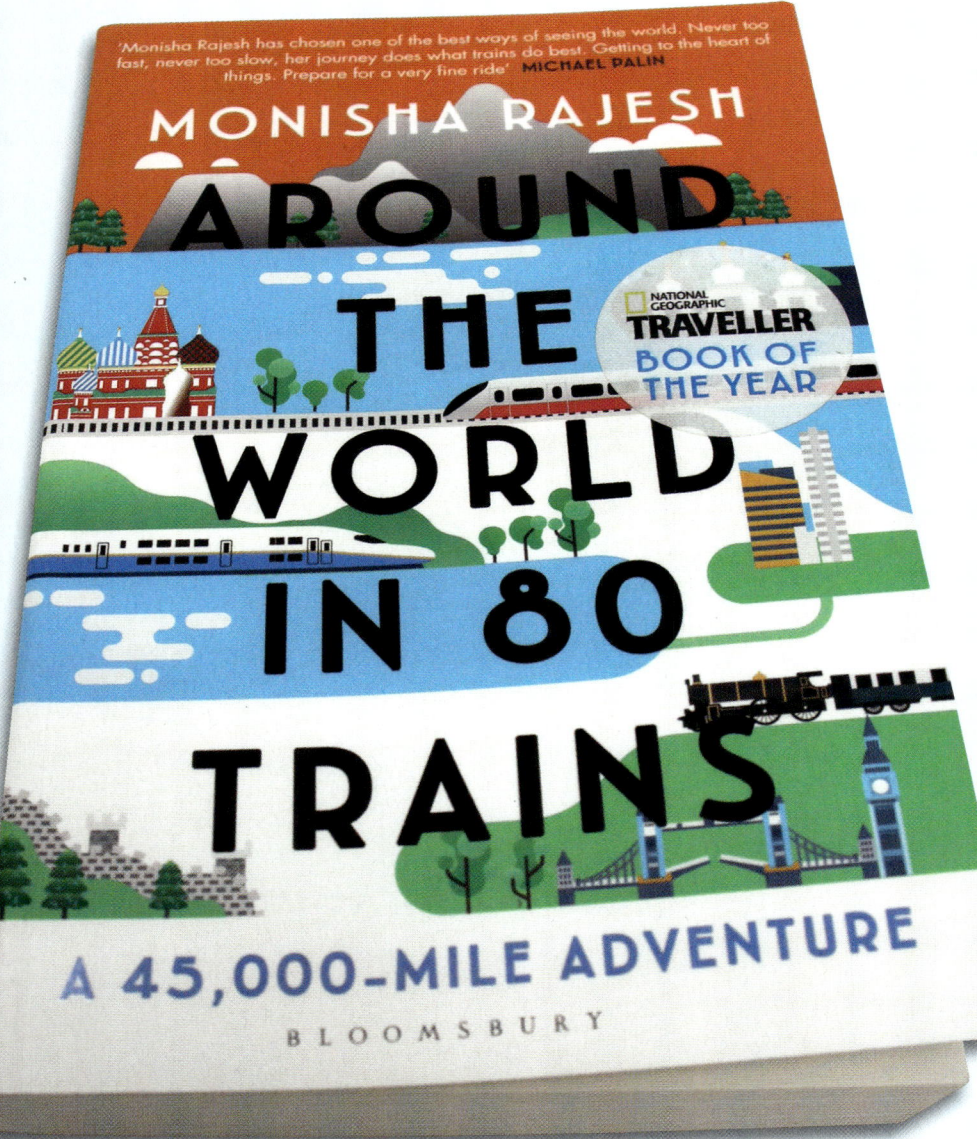

If someone has travelled 25,000 miles on 80 trains throughout India, it would be easy to believe that such an epic journey might never appeal again. Indeed, having narrowly avoided several scrapes during the trip, the author of this book swore, on her return, that she would never again take on anything so ambitious.

However, in Monisha Rajesh's own words: "Little did I know that the railways had followed me home - their dust in my hair, their rhythm in my bones, their charm infused in my blood. It had become a sickness, one that had no cure – at least no cure that I could find in London - I had to get back on the rails."

It was, therefore inevitable that despite holding down a good job in as sub editor of The Week magazine, and boyfriend Jeremy (Jem) having become her fiancé, Monisha found herself planning an even more ambitious rail journey, one that would entail her travelling throughout Europe, Lithuania, Latvia, Russia, Mongolia, China, Tibet, North Korea, Japan, Vietnam, Thailand, Malaysia and Kazakhstan – with a quick diversion for America and Canada. A journey totalling some 45,000 miles (72,420km) – the same distance as twice around the world - on another 80 trains. Jem, her fiancé of just a few months, had agreed to accompany her for a month – in the end he accompanied her for the whole journey.

Their odyssey started from St Pancras station on the Eurostar service and ended back in in London seven months later. Monisha's book is an eloquence of experiences and encounters with people she met, from all walks of life, on the trains as well as in the shops, restaurants, hotel lobbies, temples, markets and streets, throughout each of the countries visited, in what was a modern equivalent of 'the grand tour'- without the acquisitions.

STORIES GOOD AND BAD

Her exceptional powers of description reveal themselves throughout the book - embracing the landscapes she witnessed, the conversations she held, and her personal observations made throughout the journey. Monisha's recall of a deeply interesting conversation held with a seasoned Japanese Geisha. An oxygen-deprived journey by train through the Himalayas that climbed to a height of 12,100ft (3,700m) to reach Tibet. And her feelings as she discovered the depth of oppression China exerts on the people of that mountain nation. The friendly but uneasy relationship she and Jem formed with the guides appointed to accompany them on their travels by train around North Korea. These are just a few examples of a fascinating collection of stories told with humour and good grace.

Having endured travelling on a diverse mix of trains for some 44,170 miles (71,084km) around the world, they chose to make the final 830 miles (1,335km), in the guaranteed comfort of the Venice Simplon - Orient - Express. Why not? But it was during this journey that Jem discovered, to their dismay, that this was not the 80th train journey, but the 79th! You had better buy the book to discover how it justifies the title. **GW**

First published: 2019 by Bloomsbury Publishing
Price: £10.99 (paperback)
ISBN: 978 1 4088 6977 2

TRAIN *TRAVELLER* **GREAT BRITAIN – SPOTLIGHT ON WALES**

COVERING AN AREA OF JUST OVER 8,000 SQUARE MILES, WALES IS STEEPED IN HISTORY AND WHEN IT COMES TO SCENERY, THE PRINCIPALITY PACKS A MIGHTY PUNCH.

MAGICAL, MYSTICAL WALES

You would struggle to find anywhere else in the United Kingdom, possibly Europe, that offers such a diversity of landscape in so compact a package. It encapsulates mountains, lakes, estuaries, rolling countryside, rivers to rival the Highlands, pretty villages, enticing towns and 1,680 miles of coastline boasting some fabulous beaches. At one time Wales hosted more than 600 castles making it one of the most fortified countries, per square mile, in Europe. Today, only around a hundred remain but they are all worth visiting. Aside from the stunning scenery and historic buildings, Wales can also lay claim to quite possibly the finest collection of privately-run heritage narrow-gauge railways in Europe. And to make things even more appealing to those of us that just love trains, there are over 1,000 miles (1,600km) of mainline railway and more under development, so many of Wales' attractions are easily accessible by train.

Responsibility for the railways in Wales was devolved to the Welsh Government in 2005/6. Arriva Trains Wales, a subsidiary of Deutsche Bahn, who operated the franchise, worked closely with the Welsh Government to develop the current Wales and Borders network, which included the reintroduction of passenger services on what were freight-only lines in the Vale of Glamorgan and Ebbw Vale.

Following Arriva Trains Wales decision to withdraw from the bidding process to renew their franchise in 2018, joint French owned Keolis and Spanish owned Amey won the franchise and took over in October 2018. Then came COVID-19. KeolisAmey handed the franchise back to TfW but the programme of improvements planned was continued by TfW and at the time of publication most are on track for completion. You could say Wales now boasts two of the UK's three Local Railway Partnerships between train operator and Network Rail to put a more localised focus on delivering for customers.

So, all looks good for the future of rail travel in Wales. The principality is served by several rail hubs – as you would expect the principal one is in Cardiff while two are in England. Shrewsbury is central to three major Wales and the Borders' routes, as well as providing connections to Birmingham and Manchester, Chester provides links to two Wales and the Borders' routes as well as providing connections to Crew and Manchester. Newport acts as the southern terminus for the Welsh Marches Line and Swansea acts as a hub for the Heart of Wales Line and the South West Wales Line. Many of the routes in Wales have been given names that not only sound appealing but also are also extremely useful when planning a journey. Here are a few examples of the many opportunities to enjoy travelling through this superb region by train. All this information is based on Transport for Wales services. Other cross-border main-line operators also serve some of the key destinations but offer limited stops.

THE MARCHES LINE
This name is derived from the Welsh Marches through which it travels, an area that forms the borderland

ABOVE LEFT | *Betws-y-Coed Station on the Conwy Valley Line.* ROBERT MANN

LEFT | *Pont Briwet bridge over the Afon Dwyryd.* CAMBRIAN RAIL PARTNERSHIP

BELOW LEFT | *Harlech station.* CAMBRIAN RAIL PARTNERSHIP

TRAIN TRAVELLER GREAT BRITAIN - SPOTLIGHT ON WALES

ABOVE | *The remains of Cricceith Castle.*
CAMBRIAN RAIL PARTNERSHIP

between England and Wales. To be frank, the train spends most of its 84-mile (135km) journey between Newport and Shrewsbury on the English side of the border. But what a border! From Newport, the line heads north to the small market town of Abergavenny, named in 2017 as one of the best places to live in Wales. It is surrounded almost entirely by the Brecon Beacons and the Black Mountains.

The line then crosses over the border into England and continues north towards the cathedral city of Hereford on the River Wye. As well as spending an interesting day looking round the splendid choice of shops in the city, you can make a connection by train to Worcester and Birmingham from here. The lovely market town of Leominster is next - surprisingly, there is no Minster in Leominster. Next stop is the historic medieval market town of Ludlow. Described by poet laureate Sir John Betjeman as "probably the loveliest town in England", it was once in Wales when, under Henry VII, Ludlow castle acted as the headquarters for the Council of Wales and served as the administration centre for Wales and the Welsh Marches, during which time the town was effectively the capital of Wales. The 'Ludlow Marches Food and Drink Festival', is reputed to be one of the best in the UK.

Still on the English side of the border, the line continues north towards the small village of Craven Arms that serves as a junction for the Marches Line and the Heart of Wales Line. Before arriving at Craven Arms, you pass Stokesay Castle, considered to be one of finest surviving fortified manor houses in England. Last stop but one before Shrewsbury is the market town of Church Stretton that was once a busy health resort. To the east of the town is Long Mynd, a magnificent heath and moorland plateau that forms part of the Shropshire Hills and a designated Area of Outstanding Natural Beauty. In Victorian Times it was known as 'Little Switzerland'.

Finally, you reach the vibrant town of Shrewsbury, the birthplace of Charles Darwin. Almost encircled by the River Severn, it boasts an unspoilt medieval town centre plan, a castle, great shops and more than 660 listed buildings. Here you can connect with the Cambrian Line, the Heart of Wales Line and the North Wales Coast Line as well as make a connection that will take you on to Manchester via Crewe.

BORDERLANDS

Sometimes referred to as the Mid-Wirral line, the **Borderlands Line** is a short route that runs between Wrexham and the village of Bidston in the new county of Merseyside on the Wirral Peninsula. Interestingly, Wrexham recognised as the largest town in north Wales, is now a city and is situated between the Welsh mountains and the lower Dee Valley, close to the English-Welsh border. From Wrexham the line travels through the hills of northeast Wales into Flintshire, stopping at the small town of Buckley and then Shotton, where a connection to the North Wales Coast Line can be made. The line then crosses over the famous Hawarden swing bridge spanning the tidal River Dee that flows between England and Wales. Sadly, the swing bridge no longer swings as it has been welded up so tall ships can no longer ply the River Dee! Close by you will find the relatively new Hawarden Castle, a mansion house that was built close to the remains of Hawarden Old Castle in 1752. Its occupants have included Sir John Glynne, 6th Baronet and the liberal politician William Gladstone. In 1896 the Archbishop of Canterbury died at the castle and his body was put on a train at nearby Sandycroft Station (which is on the North Wales Coast Line) to be returned to London.

The Grade I listed medieval Hawarden Old Castle featured at a pivotal point during the Welsh struggle for independence in the 13th century. In 1282, Dafydd ap Gruffydd attacked Hawarden Castle in what turned out to be the final Welsh conflict with Norman England, during which Welsh independence was lost. In these more peaceful times, on arrival at the delightful village of Bidston you can connect with the Wirral Line - a Merseyrail network that takes you to Liverpool.

TWO HERITAGE RAILWAYS

The **Chester to Shrewsbury Line** travels through three counties and some fine scenery as it traverses the northern tip of the Welsh Marches. Although in England (only just) Chester's Roman walls, medieval shop fronts and superb shops and restaurants are well worth exploring. From Chester the first stop is Wrexham located just across the border of Wales, followed by the small village of Ruabon. Here you can catch a bus that takes you to Llangollen where there is a heritage railway, horse-drawn canal boats and the mighty 126-foot high Pontcysyllte Aqueduct that carries the Llangollen canal over the River Dee. The railway station was once a junction for the now closed Ruabon to Barmouth line, sections of which are now run by the restored Llangollen Railway, Bala Lake Railway (now narrow-gauge) and as part of the Mawddach Cycle Trail. The last stop before Shrewsbury is the small village of Gobowen, just two miles from the attractive market town of Oswestry where the Cambrian Heritage Railway Trust and Society is based in a newly restored Oswestry Railway Station. Oswestry was once connected to Gobowen by a small branch line – but guess who recommended its closure?

TO THE ISLE OF ANGLESEY

The **North Wales Coast Line** links Chester to the ferry port in Holyhead on the Isle of Anglesey. Leaving Chester, it travels along the picturesque Irish Sea coast of North Wales calling at several stations along the coast including Flint, which lies on the estuary of the River Dee, the popular seaside towns of Prestatyn, Rhyl and Colwyn Bay, followed by Llandudno - by far the largest of the seaside towns in North Wales. Llandudno, with its two shores and a pier, is an extremely handsome town with impressive architecture designed by George Felton and built between 1857 and 1877. Much of the town is still owned by the Mostyn Estate and its appearance is strongly upheld by rigid controls, as is the general development of the town. Llandudno developed as a resort alongside the Great Orme peninsular, a major tourist attraction that protrudes northwards into the Irish Sea and reaches a height of 679ft (207m). Mostly owned by Mostyn Estates, the limestone peninsular is home to several large herds of wild Kashmiri goats descended from a pair given to Lord Mostyn by Queen Victoria. The famous Great Orme cable Tramway and the Llandudno Cable Car both carry passengers to and from Llandudno to the top of the Great Orme (Danish for Sea Monster) where there is a visitor centre and fantastic views along the coast. From Llandudno Junction station you can also join the **Conwy Valley Line** that connects the North Wales Coast Line to Blaenau Ffestiniog in the heart of Snowdonia, now called Eryri - more about this line later.

ABOVE | *A new Class 231 at Aber station on the Rhymney line.* ROBERT MANN

LEFT | *The elegant curved Cynghordy Viaduct from below.* K WEST

TRAIN TRAVELLER GREAT BRITAIN – SPOTLIGHT ON WALES

The last stop on the mainland is the cathedral and university city of Bangor, located alongside the Menai Strait that separates the mainland from the Isle of Anglesey. It claims to be the oldest city in Wales and boasts the longest shopping street in Wales. You can get a bus here to the Snowdonia Mountain Railway via Llanberis. From Bangor the train crosses over the Menai Strait via the famous Britannia Bridge. The original bridge, designed by Robert Stephenson, was built exclusively for the passage of trains. During the design stage the Admiralty insisted that it had to be high enough for a fully rigged 'man-o-war' to pass through before they agreed to sanction it. In 1970 it suffered a disastrous fire that was so extensive it was considered un-repairable. The bridge has since been rebuilt using the same piers but is now a two-tier bridge carrying both trains and road traffic.

Llanfairpwllgwyngyllgogerychwyrndrobwllllantysilio-gogogoch is the most famous station on the Isle of Anglesey, if not all of Wales. However, the name was created by the Victorians for the benefit of tourists and has no historical basis – the station's real name is simply Llanfairpwll. The destination is of course Holyhead, the largest town on the island and a seaport where you can board a Stena Line ferry to Dublin.

NARROW GAUGE NIRVANA

RIGHT | *The Welsh Highland Railway in the Aberglaslyn Pass.*
CROWN COPYRIGHT

The **Conwy Valley Line** is one of the best-kept secrets in all of Wales. It connects Llandudno Junction on the north coast of Wales to Blaenau Ffestiniog in the Eryri National Park (formerly Snowdonia). Built originally to carry slate from the Ffestiniog quarries to a specially built quay for export by sea, the 27-mile journey travels through breath taking landscapes, skirts the imposing 12th century Dolwyddelan Castle and passes through ancient quarries, tracks, forests and the high peaks of Eryri. With Conwy Castle on your right, overlooking the picturesque Conwy Bay estuary, the line heads south along the banks of the Afon (river) Conwy all the way to its confluence with the turbulent Afon Lledr near Betws-y-Coed. Here it crosses the Lledr on the impressive Gethin's viaduct and then enters the longest single-track railway tunnel in the UK. It is an impressive 2.2 miles (3.5km) long and reaches a height of 790ft (240m) above sea level midway through. Exiting the tunnel, the line emerges into a dramatic world of blue slate at Bleaenau Ffestiniog, the centre of Wales' famous slate quarrying and mining industry. You can continue your journey from here on the delightful Ffestiniog narrow gauge railway to Porthmadog that sits at the foot of the Eryri National Park, alongside the Afon Glaslyn estuary and close to the world-famous Portmeirion fantasy Italian village created by Clough Williams-Ellis. As well as serving the Cambrian Line, Porthmadog station is a narrow gauge enthusiast's nirvana as it also acts as a 'port' to two famous narrow gauge railways, the Ffestiniog Railway, the world's oldest working narrow gauge railway, and the Welsh Highland Railway, the UK's longest narrow gauge railway (25 miles [40km]). The Welsh Highland Railway travels to Caernarfon, where you can see another world famous medieval Castle, and catch a bus to the Snowdonia Mountain Railway. At one time Caernarfon had five railway stations and was once connected to the main-line network. Today, it is served only by the Welsh Highland Railway that interestingly travels in the middle of one of the roads in the town to reach its terminus right under the Castle! It would be remiss of us not the mention a little about Caernarfon Castle since, in a land of castles it is the most impressive in the Principality and where Prince Charles was invested as Prince of Wales. In the opinion of military historian Allen Brown, should the firing galleries along the northern face ever have been completed, it would have been 'one of the most formidable concentrations of fire-power to be found in the Middle Ages'.

All the stops on the Conwy Valley Line are request stops. For more detailed information on the above narrow-gauge railways, plus three other Welsh narrow-gauge railways (including the Snowdonia Mountain Railway), we recommend you track down a copy of a book called *Small Island by Little Train* by Chris Arnot.

CROSS COUNTRY

The **Cambrian Line** travels through a wonderful mix of rural Welsh landscape. From the rolling, border hills that surround the market towns of Welshpool and Newtown, this line runs through the northern reaches of the Cambrian Mountains (source of the Rivers Severn and Wye just two

miles apart) to Caersws, a quiet village community located approximately halfway between Shrewsbury and Aberystwyth on the banks of the fledgling River Severn. The next stop is Machynlleth, referred to colloquially as Mach. This ancient market town - its royal charter goes back to Edward 1 in 1291 - is where Owain Glyndŵr was crowned Prince of Wales in 1404. Machynlleth is also where Laura Ashley opened her first shop in 1961 and is home to the Welsh Museum of Modern Art. Between 1859 and 1948, the town was served by the narrow gauge Corris Railway which carried slate from nearby quarries. This has since been re-opened by a group of enthusiasts as a delightful preserved railway that runs between Corris village and Maespoeth in the Dulas Valley. Known as the Rheilffordd Corris Railway there are plans to extend its' reach to Tan y Coed Forest Amenity site.

Leaving Machynlleth, the route follows the beautiful Afon Dyfi valley, host to the Dyfi National Nature Reserve. Just four miles beyond Machynlleth at Dovey Junction (Dyfi Junction), the line splits into two with one heading south to terminate at Aberystwyth and the other heading north to

terminate at Pwllheli on the Llŷn Peninsula. The estuary area of this river is home to some of the finest landscapes and wildlife areas in Europe and is also recognised as a UNESCO Biosphere Reserve.

Taking the northern route, the first stop is Tywyn, where the delightful Talyllyn narrow gauge railway is based. The line then heads over an impressive causeway that reaches across the stunning Mawddach Estuary to the beautiful seaside resort of Barmouth. Next stop is the small seaside resort of Harlech guarded by the spectacular Grade I listed

medieval Harlech Castle built on top of a spur of rock overlooking the coast. UNESCO considers Harlech Castle to be one of 'the finest examples of late 13th century and early 14th century military architecture in Europe and is classed as a World Heritage site. Continuing north, the line travels over the famous Cob, built across the sands of Afon Glaslyn estuary to the busy rail hub of Porthmadog. Criccieth is next where the remains of yet another Welsh Castle can be seen sitting on a headland between two beaches. The final destination is Pwllheli, a small market town located on the eastern edge of the Llŷn Peninsula.

Back to Dyfi Junction. The southbound route takes you to Aberystwyth via Borth, an unusual seaside village resort that appears wide open to the elements. However, it offers all the trappings of a seaside destination including Blue Flag status, toilets, cafes, restaurants, pubs, shops, parking, and lifeguard services. The village and the railway station formed the backdrop to the main storyline in season one, episode four of Hinterland – The Girl in the Water. This dark, Welsh TV production was screened in 2013 and reviews of the episode make mention of Borth and the surrounding beach and marshlands. And, as another claim to fame for Borth, in 1876 the entire Uppingham School from Rutland, England, consisting of 300 boys, 30 masters and their families, moved to Borth for a period of 14 months, taking over the disused Cambrian Hotel and a large number of boarding houses to avoid a typhoid epidemic in the school town.

A brand new station at Bow Street, just a few miles north of Aberystwyth has recently been completed close to the site of the original station that closed in the mid-1960s. It is the first to be built by Transport for Wales. The final stop is the ancient market town and seaside resort of Aberystwyth. A major Welsh educational centre, its university has a student population of more than 10,000 and is where Prince Charles studied the Welsh language.

The arrival of the railway in 1864 coincided with the opening of its 952ft (292m) long pier. These two events kicked off a Victorian tourist boom with the town once billed as the 'Biarritz of Wales'. As well as the pier and a handsome curved promenade - often pounded mercilessly by the sea - Aberystwyth has a funicular cliff railway and is home to the splendid Vale of Rheidol narrow gauge railway.

JEWEL IN THE CROWN

The Heart of Wales Line is deservedly rated as one of the most scenic in the UK. More pastoral in nature than England's rugged Settle to Carlisle line or Scotland's West Highland line, it runs for 121 miles between Shrewsbury and Swansea on the South Wales coast. Leaving Shrewsbury, it travels through the Welsh Marches to the towns of Church Stretton and Craven Arms, before swinging southwest to traverse diagonally across ➔

LEFT | *The stunning Mawddach Estuary and the impressive Barmouth railway Bridge. It's possible to walk or cycle across this 150 year old wooden bridge. On the Tywyn side of the bridge is the delightful Fairbourne narrow-gauge railway that runs between Tywyn, Fairbourne, and Dolgellau and the terminus for the Talylllyn railway.* ROBERT MANN

LEFT | *The tram climbing the Great Orme.* G WEST

TRAIN TRAVELLER GREAT BRITAIN - SPOTLIGHT ON WALES

ABOVE | *The Ffestiniog Railway steam train arriving at Tan y Bwlch station.* CROWN COPYRIGHT

RIGHT | *Llandrindod Wells station on the Heart of Wales Line.* ROBERT MANN

South Wales through mile after mile of verdant rolling hills to the small market town of Knighton. Perversely, part of the town of Knighton is in Powys, Wales, and the other part, including the railway station is in Shropshire, England! Historically, the whole of Knighton was once in England being east of Offa's Dyke, the ancient border between the two countries.

Further south the line serves three spa towns. First is Llandrindod Wells, a handsome town boasting superb examples of Victorian and Edwardian architecture, independent artisan shops and good hotels. The second spa town is Builth Wells that lies in a flood plain at the confluence of the Rivers Wye and Irfon. Builth is home to the Royal Welsh Agricultural showground and the Royal Welsh Show but it is worth noting that the station for Builth Wells is located at Llanelwedd, two miles to the north of the town. The third spa town is Llanwrtyd Wells, one of Britain's smallest towns with a population of just over 850 people and famous for founding and holding the World Bog Snorkelling championships. It is well worth alighting at any of these towns for a short stay over.

Just south of Llanwrtyd is the remote Sugar Loaf railway station. This request stop is for those who wish to walk or cycle to the prominent knoll known as the Sugar Loaf, the highest point in the area at 1955ft (596m.). For the next few miles, the line travels through its most spectacular sections before approaching the elegant eighteen arch Cynghordy viaduct, a 102ft (30.5m) high curved structure that stretches across the pretty Afon Bran Valley. There is another request stop at the village of Cynghordy for those wishing to view this engineering masterpiece from below. From the top of the viaduct there are stunning panoramic views of the verdant valley and surroundings. This is also close to where the line reaches its highest point of 820ft (250m). Leaving Cynghordy station you enter a 1,000-yard (915m) tunnel cut through the surrounding hills before descending steadily for 8.5miles (13.7km) towards the market town of Llandovery. In the past they used pusher engines to ascend this 1in 60gradient.

A gateway to the Brecon Beacons, the market town of Llandovery boasts one of the line's finest station buildings. Its welcoming café is a popular place for walkers to warm up in front of the log burner in winter or for summer visitors to take refreshment and a browse through the Heart of Wales Line archives on display. Close to Llandovery is also where you will find 'Llwynywermod', the official Welsh home of Prince Charles and the Duchess of Cornwall. The remains of Llandovery Castle are in the town centre, where King Henry IV made use of it whilst on a sortie in Wales when he rounded up Llywelyn ap Gruffydd Fychan and had him executed quite gruesomely in the town's market place for leading the

king's army on a 'wild goose chase' under the pretence of taking them to a secret rebels' camp to ambush Glyndŵr's forces. He was half-hanged, disembowelled while alive, beheaded, and quartered - the quarters then salted and dispatched to other Welsh towns for public display! There is a fine 16ft high stainless steel monument of him close by to where he was executed.

Leaving Llandovery, the line travels close to the banks of the River Tywi, the longest river that flows entirely within Wales. Keeping a lookout, you might be lucky to see red kites flying as this is close to one of their official feeding centres, before you arrive at the small town of Llandeilo. The next stop on the line is Ammanford located in Carmarthenshire, followed by Pontardulais. The countryside changes quite significantly from here as the train descends towards the salt marshes of the Loughor Estuary where anyone can collect one bucketful of cockles! The River Loughor, fed from an underground lake in the Black Mountains acts as the border between Carmarthenshire and Swansea. You can alight at Llanelli if you wish to join the South West Wales line and head west for Carmarthenshire and Pembrokeshire, or you can continue on to enjoy the bustling city of Swansea, the official end - or beginning - of the splendid Heart of Wales Line.

GLORIOUS SOUTH WEST WALES

The **South West Wales Line** connects the urban heartlands of Swansea to Carmarthenshire and glorious Pembrokeshire. Beyond Llanelli, the largest town in the county of Carmarthenshire, the train follows the contours of Carmarthen Bay, stopping at several small villages en route, such as Kidwelly and Ferryside before arriving at the busy walled county town of Carmarthen. Legend has it that Merlin was born in a cave close to Carmarthen. Legend also has it that if a tree called 'Merlin's Oak' were to fall it would signal the downfall of the town. To prevent this from happening the tree in question was dug up when it died in 1978 and a fragment of it placed in the town's museum.

Just beyond the small town of Whitland, where the ruins of a Cistercian Abbey that predates Tintern Abbey are still visible, the line divides into two. The southbound line heads for Pembroke Dock, but calls first at the small resort of Tenby - rated one of the most beautiful, walled harbour towns and seaside resorts in the UK. Its unique collection of colourfully painted Georgian buildings and medieval castle overlook two glorious beaches, a small, busy working harbour, Carmarthen Bay, and the holy island of Caldey that is still occupied and run by a community of Cistercian monks. Beyond Tenby there are two more stops en route before the line reaches the handsome, Georgian town of Pembroke, built alongside an impressive 12th century medieval castle that overlooks the River Pembroke. The line terminates at Pembroke Dock, a small town and port where you can board the Irish Ferry service to Rosslare.

BACK TO WHITLAND

This section of the **South West Wales Line** heads west before splitting just north of Haverfordwest, with the south-bound line heading for the county town of Haverfordwest (not Pembroke as some would surmise) and the ferry port of Milford Haven - whilst the north-bound line heads for the town of Fishguard and the ferry terminal for the Stena Line service - also to Rosslare. Close by is Fishguard's Lower Town with its lovely old harbour where the last invasion of Britain (by French troops) took place in 1797 - and where Dylan Thomas' Under Milk Wood was filmed starring Richard Burton.

From the towns of Pembroke, Haverfordwest and Fishguard you can access the more rugged and remote parts of the stunning Pembrokeshire coastline, via bus, bike or boots – a paradise for swimmers, sunbathers, surfers, beachcombers, wildlife-watchers, outdoor adventurers and walkers for whom the 186 mile long Pembrokeshire Coastal Path, described by Lonely Planet as' one of the best long distance trails in the world' would be a magical destination.

BELOW | *Conwy Castle in North Wales.* CROWN COPYRIGHT

TRAIN TRAVELLER A HISTORY

A HISTORICAL TRAIN OF EVENTS

RIGHT I *Venice Simplon-Orient-Express coursing through the Austrian Alps.* BELMOND

BELOW I *This elegant Pullman designed drawing room car (carriage) was built in Detroit, and then shipped to the UK and reassembled by the Midland Railway Company in Derby and named Albion - circa 1870s.* ALAMY

You could say George Mortimer Pullman was an American visionary, engineer, industrialist, and social idealist - although on the latter point, he was, can we say, found to be wanting. Born in 1831, his first business venture specialised in raising and moving whole buildings on jack-screws (sometimes to a height of eight feet or more - with the occupants still in them) a system invented by his father to allow repairs and/or construction work to take place beneath them. Despite this highly specialised activity, in 1865 he turned his attention to the design and construction of the first luxurious railroad sleeping carriage - probably because of his uncomfortable experiences travelling vast distances by train across the USA. Called the 'Pioneer', it was a precursor to an impressive industrial and social empire that established a whole new aspirational style of travel in the process.

Not only did the Pullman Company design and build luxury railway carriages, it also owned and operated many of them in the US well into the mid-20th century. They were attached mainly to regular passenger train services operated by a variety of railroad companies of the time. Amongst many other rail innovations attributable to Pullman was the 'President', a sleeping carriage with an attached kitchen and dining car (nicknamed the 'hotel on wheels') and the 'vestibule' - a means of interconnecting individual carriages by covered gangways, previously connected via open platforms.

Pullman also exported his Pullman carriages into Europe and the UK, with the pioneering Midland Railway Company being its first UK customer in 1874. They ran the UK's first Pullman service from Bradford Forster Square to London St Pancras in 1874 and in the same year introduced a sleeper service between Glasgow and London Euston. They were also responsible for the construction of the magnificent St Pancras Station and the much heralded 'Settle to Carlisle' railway line.

A **FEUDAL** BARON

George Pullman not only created the Pullman Car Company, he also built a town called Pullman in 1880 - in the much the same vein as Sir Titus Salt who built the ➔

JOHN LEDDSOME REVEALS A FASCINATING TALE CONNECTING GEORGE PULLMAN TO GEORGES NAGELMACKERS TO DAME AGATHA CHRISTIE TO JAMES SHERWOOD – THE MAN THAT RELAUNCHED THE RENOWNED BELMOND VENICE SIMPLON-ORIENT-EXPRESS.

TRAIN *TRAVELLER* *A HISTORY*

RIGHT | *Sleeping cabin on the Venice Simplon-Orient-Express.* BELMOND

RIGHT CENTRE | *South Eastern Railway- London to Constantinople Orient Express Poster.* ARCHIVE

> *"If their mistresses were unavailable for a journey, Wagon Lits' cabin-staff were charged with the procurement of suitable companions for the journey!"*

village of Saltaire, near Bradford in 1853. Located adjacent to his manufacturing plant, Pullman believed that "the country air and fine facilities, without agitators, saloons and city vice districts, would result in a happy, loyal workforce." Incorporating housing, shops, theatres, parks, churches, a hotel, a library and even a man-made lake - all for his employees, it attracted both nationwide and worldwide attention.

However, this social enterprise was not without its problems, and Pullman, disposed towards imposing draconian rules upon his tenants and workforce, was accused of acting like a 'feudal baron'. Following a period of confrontational labour disputes, resulting in the death of some 30 workers, the town of Pullman, on the orders of the Supreme Court of Illinois, became a neighbourhood of Chicago. Despite his shortcomings George Pullman was unquestionably the catalyst to a fascinating train of events that lead right up to present times.

Another George - actually Georges Nagelmackers - was born in Belgium in 1845, the son of a family of bankers. Georges, however, chose to avoid the banking profession and trained instead as an engineer. Whilst on a visit to the USA in 1869, he must have travelled extensively on trains that had Pullman dining and sleeping carriages attached.

Although there are no records to confirm that this exposure to the Pullman carriages influenced his long-term ambition, he was undoubtedly impressed by them. Soon after returning to Belgium he formed Compagnie Internationale de Wagons-Lits (CIWL). This was at a time when several pan-European trains were already running, which in turn attracted the attention and active involvement of several influential European bankers, most notably the Rothschilds.

BOUGHT BACK CONTROL

Georges Nagelmackers' ambition was to establish a fleet of luxury trains incorporating sleeping and dining cars for pan-European travel, his aim being to run a bi-weekly service between Paris and Constantinople (now Istanbul) that he called the 'Express of the Orient'. He purchased several Pullman cars for his early ventures that were attached to existing rail service trains, in similar style to Pullman in the US. CIWL endured a plethora of financial and operational obstacles, including more than one change of ownership and management before Georges finally bought back control, aided no doubt by his banking connections. He then went on to launch, amongst a number of other services, what we now recognise as 'The Orient Express' in 1883. This name should not be confused with the Venice Simplon-Orient-Express that took to the rails in 1982, which is a private, luxury cruise train modelled on the 'Orient Express' but most definitely not a service train.

The original 'Express of the Orient' ran first between Paris and Giurgiu in Romania, and then finally between Paris and Constantinople. Although this service faced a few teething problems, it eventually became a success, attracting a host of wealthy and aristocratic passengers including several crowned heads of Europe. Among the royal clients were King Leopold II of Belgium (who also happened to head the list of CIWL investors) and Carol II of Romania. They often travelled with their mistresses - and if their mistresses were unavailable for a journey, Wagons Lits' cabin staff were charged with the procurement of suitable companions for the journey! In later years, 1928 to be precise, it also attracted the patronage of no less a person than (Dame) Agatha Christie, writer of arguably one of the world's most famous novels - Murder on the Orient Express.

CARRIAGE BLOWN UP

The Orient Express service was inevitably interrupted and re-routed several times during both World wars. It also played an unexpected role when Germany's surrender to the Allies at the end of World War One was performed in a Lits carriage at Compiégne. In an act of theatrical revenge, Hitler ordered the same carriage to be delivered to the same spot for the French to surrender to him in June 1940, and then had the carriage put on display in Berlin. When the war turned in favour of the Allies in 1944 Hitler, fearing humiliation, ordered the carriage to be destroyed!

LEFT | *Sumptuous bar interior of the Venice Simplon-Orient-Express.*
BELMOND

TRAIN TRAVELLER A HISTORY

Following World War Two, the creation of the Iron Curtain, the devastated economies of Europe and the unexpected growth of air travel, the Orient Express service entered a long and steady decline, and by the end of the 1970s had ceased to exist in all but name. Using the same name, the service continued to run nightly between Paris and Bucharest, which was later cut back to Strasbourg and Vienna. But by 2009 even this route was removed from the timetables, a victim then of the introduction of high-speed trains.

However, Agatha Christie's famous novel, first published in 1934 and made into a film in 1974 and then remade in 2017, has been seared into the subconscious of the public ever since. This, no doubt contributed in no small measure towards the emergence and success of the Venice Simplon-Orient-Express - a brand created and owned by luxury hotel and rail travel company Belmond.

DILAPIDATED SLEEPING CARS

The story behind the creation of the Venice Simplon-Orient Express centres on Kentucky born James Sherwood, who died earlier this year. Sherwood made his first fortune from Sea Containers, a marine leasing company he founded in 1965. At the age of just 36 he floated Sea Containers on the New York Stock Exchange, becoming a multi-millionaire in the process. This freed him to devote his time and money on two obsessions - hotels and trains.

> "...the creation of the Iron Curtain, the devastated economies of Europe and the unexpected growth of air travel, the Orient Express service entered a long and steady decline"

Having purchased and restored the Hotel Cipriani in Venice, and aware of the British obsession for historic trains and their love for Venice - no doubt influenced by Agatha Christie's timeless novel - he came up with the idea of sourcing and restoring original Orient Express carriages and running them as a private luxury train - first from London to Paris, and then Paris to Venice - with the passengers ending up at his Hotel Cipriani.

To set this idea in motion he purchased two dilapidated first-class sleeping cars dating back to the 1920s at a Sotheby's auction in Monte Carlo. The carriages had once formed part of the original Orient Express set. Interestingly, the King of Morocco also purchased two of five that were up for auction that day, for his royal train.

James Sherwood then proceeded to track down a further 25 original carriages, some of which had been used subsequently for services other than carrying passengers - such as the transportation of racing pigeons, a garden house and even a brothel in Limoges. He then spent upwards of £20m meticulously restoring them to their original splendour.

In a 2012 interview with Elizabeth Grice in the *Daily Telegraph*, James Sherwood commented: "When I bought those two old carriages in Monte Carlo, people thought I was slightly crazy. They said it was a fun idea, but it would not work. The common wisdom was that luxury rail travel

LEFT | *The luxurious restored lounge car on Belmond's Andean Explorer that travels between Cusco and Puno a journey of 242miles (390km).* BELMOND

LEFT | *Dining in style on-board the restored carriages of the Venice Simplon-Orient Express.* BELMOND

was dead. Now it is fully booked every year and the carriages, each one different, are in better condition than they have ever been. Concorde has come and gone and the Orient-Express is still here. It was a good hunch."

Following his launch of the Venice Simplon-Orient-Express', James Sherwood went on to expand his Belmond hotel and luxury train portfolio to include 46 properties across 24 countries, encompassing three luxury safari lodges, seven luxury trains, river cruises, restaurants and exclusive package tours. That was until April 2019 when LVMH (Moët Hennessy - Louis Vuitton SE) the world's largest privately owned, luxury goods business run by Bernard Arnault (of Christian Dior notoriety) purchased Belmond outright. Taking over the baton from James Sherwood, LVMH have continued to expand and enhance the Belmond portfolio of inspirational travel experiences and destinations. Sadly, James Sherwood died aged 86 on 18th May 2020 - strange then, that his name is not mentioned in any of Belmond's current promotional literature or websites?

Because of the carriages' wooden construction, they are not allowed to travel through the Channel Tunnel, so Belmond introduced a London to Folkestone service 'The Belmond British Pullman' using some of the restored Pullman coaches for daytime use. Today, the Belmond British Pullman, made up of 11 whimisically-named authentic carriages has been re-purposed and transports its lucky passengers to destinations around the UK on day and weekend journeys. Then there is the Royal Scotsman. Running since 1985 it ranks among the world's most luxurious trains and boasts mahogany-clad coaches, and an observation deck at the rear - a rare feature on British trains - as well as a sumptuous Grand Suite that Belmond describe as 'decadent'! With accommodation for just 36 guests and 12 members of staff, it projects Edwardian elegance with country house comforts for those who can afford it. Journeys can be enjoyed on this iconic train from one to seven nights with a five-day 720 miles round trip. that rolls through the heart of the Scottish Highlands.

INSTANBUL - ALONE

Agatha Christie, born in 1890, travelled widely with her first husband, Archie Christie, but the marriage ended in 1928 when he fell in love with another woman and asked her for a divorce. Stunned by the divorce, she famously disappeared causing national alarm - only to be discovered ten days later holed up at the Swan Hotel in Harrogate, having signed in under the name of her ex-husband's lover.

Trying to put her life back together, Agatha continued to travel extensively and on the spur of the moment

TRAIN TRAVELLER A HISTORY

ABOVE | *James Sherwood, founder of Belmond and the Venice Simplon-Orient Express.* BELMOND

BELOW | *The River Dart.* VISIT DEVON

accomplished a lifelong goal by boarding the Orient Express to Istanbul - alone. She then continued on the 'Taurus Express' to Aleppo (another service created by CIWL) finally ending up in Baghdad via bus where she met Leonard Woolley, a British archaeologist who was excavating the site of Ur, an important Sumerian city-state in ancient Mesopotamia, now southern Iraq. This was the trip that inspired her to write Murder on the Orient Express.

On a second trip to Baghdad she met Wooley's young assistant Max Mallowan, they fell in love and married in 1930. Agatha loved trains and has been quoted as saying: "What can beat a train? Trains are wonderful. I well adore them. To travel by train is to see nature and human beings, towns, churches and rivers - in fact to see life." In her biography, she wrote: "Trains have always been one of my favourite things. It is sad nowadays that one no longer has engines that seem to be one's personal friends." Murder on the Orient Express was not her only book to feature a train in the plot, she also wrote The Mystery of the Blue Train (published before Murder on the Orient Express), The Girl In The Train and The 4.50 from Paddington.

GREENWAY HALT

In 1938 Agatha and Max Mallowan purchased the Greenway House Estate in Devon as a summer residence. Although living primarily in London they had previously owned a summer residence in Torquay. She described Greenway as "the loveliest place in the world" - and who can argue with that. Set high on the banks of the beautiful River Dart one wonders if the proximity of the railway line that threads its way between the River Dart and the edges of the estate was an added attraction. At the time of their purchase Great Western Railway ran this branch line that connected Paignton to Kingswear.

Agatha Christie would no doubt have been thrilled to learn that the Dartmouth Steam Railway & River Co, the local heritage railway company who now run this line, built a station in 2012 at the foot of the estate called Greenway Halt to give visitors access to The Greenway House Estate. The estate itself was purchased from members of the Christie family by the National Trust in 2000.

If you were to try and decide who was the most influential person in this train of events, who would it be? Would it be George Pullman, the originator of the Pullman sleeping and dining carriages? Would it be Georges Nagelmackers who saw the potential of a cross-European network of trains offering exciting destinations with comfortable sleeping and dining facilities for his passengers? Would it be Agatha Christie, a notorious fan of trains, for penning Murder on The Orient Express? Or would it be James Sherwood for realising the potential of the public's appetite for luxurious travel by train and investing his money in the restoration and re-incarnation of an aspirational dream?

Footnote

Andrew Eames wrote a fascinating book called *The 8.55 to Baghdad* (winner of the 2004 British Guild of Travel Writers Narrative Travel Book of the Year Award) that records his personal endeavour to retrace Agatha Christie's journey on the Orient Express - starting from the village of Sunningdale where she lived for a while, and ending up in Baghdad, via Aleppo - on the eve of the Iraq War! For anyone interested in Agatha Christie and train travel, this book is a must - if you can track down a copy!

BOOK REVIEW

ANGLO SCOTTISH SLEEPERS - *DAVID MEARA*

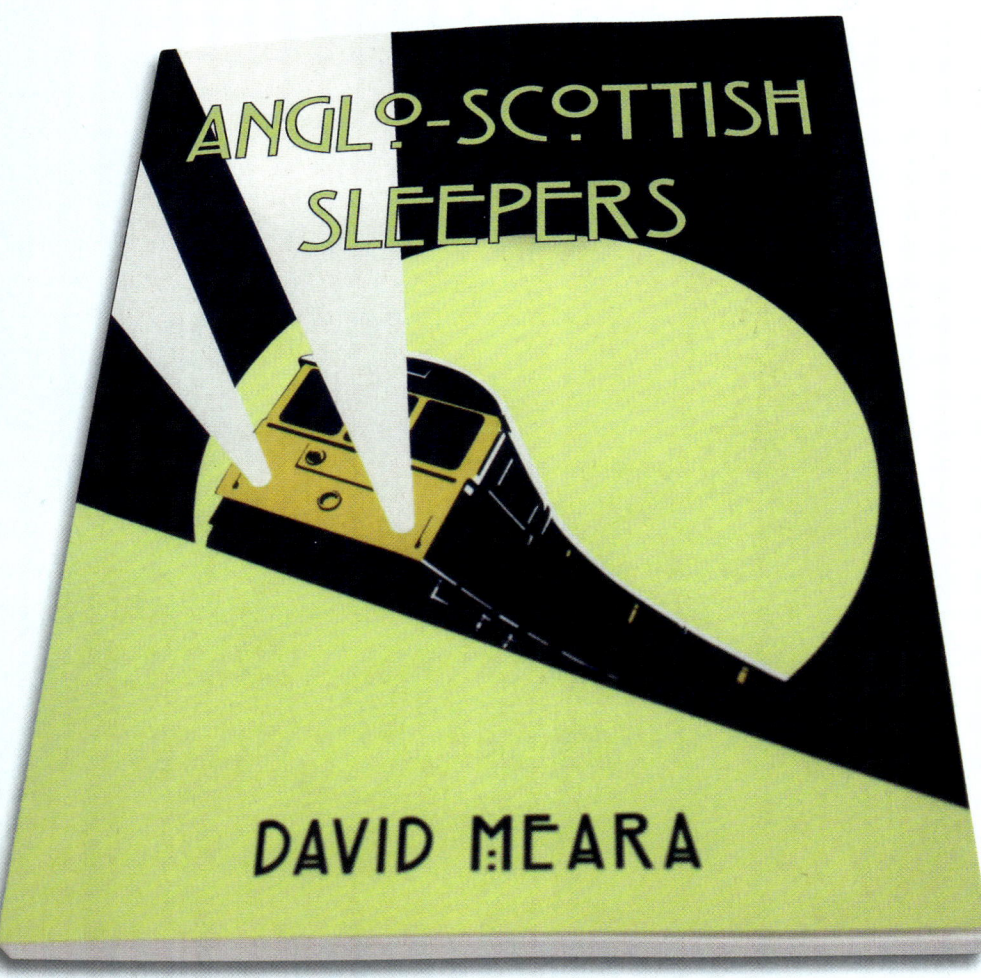

At the very beginning of his book *Anglo Scottish Sleepers*, David Meara, a retired British Anglican priest, expresses his surprise and obvious delight that providing sleeper services in Britain remains a key part of our rail network, underscored by the recent introduction of a fleet of new sleeper carriages by for the Caledonian Sleeper service. And this, despite the haphazard evolution of such services in Britain dating back to 1873.

His enthusiasm and obvious expertise on the subject, clearly stems from his experience when he first boarded an overnight service on a relief train in 1959, travelling in an old third-class, four-berth compartment. This book however, is not just about the Anglo-Scottish sleeper, but a history of sleeper services in the British Isles in general, including the London to Penzance sleeper service (which still runs) as well as the 'Motorail' services which run no more.

David's book covers all bases. If your interest is in the rolling stock - then there are drawings, illustrations, and photographs of some of the earliest known sleeper carriages, including the very earliest known dating back to 1873. Other illustrations and drawings show surprisingly luxurious accommodation available in the late Victorian and Edwardian eras, together with photographs of more modern designs used on the Caledonian Sleeper service just prior to the introduction of their new fleet.

If your interest is more nostalgic, then there are equally lots of historical photographs of iconic advertising posters, graphics, and social scenes. Certainly, David's narrative hints at his regret of the lost glory days of train travel when, for example, dining cars had British Rail-branded cutlery. He backs this up by saying: "I have watched the fortunes of the service rise and fall, and then in this century rise again as we have become disenchanted with long-distance car travel or the hassle of airports and flying."

One reason for this, suggests David, "is that the anticipation of the journey is rivalled only by the prospect of enjoying unlikely liaisons as the service's greatest pull... people become more confiding, secure in the knowledge that they probably won't meet again!" Supporting this theory, David's book is peppered with personal anecdotes and amusing stories gleaned from generations of passengers who have used the sleepers over many years. For instance, he recounts the story of one female passenger who "after partaking in a few drams with a lively crowd in the lounge car, retired to a gentleman's cabin. When she awoke, she discovered that the Highland sleeper had divided overnight; she ended up in Aberdeen, whilst her luggage went on to Fort William where her 'irate' husband was waiting on the platform".

Another anecdote involved the famous author and artist Beatrix Potter. Travelling from King's Cross to Perth via Edinburgh in the summer of 1892, she was accompanied by her pet rabbit, Benjamin. "Benjamin Bunny travelled in a covered basket in the wash-place," Potter noted in her journal. "Took him out of the basket near Dunbar, but proved scared and bit the family." David's book is full of wonderful stories like these although, one or two are a little unsavoury!

David argues that the sleeper service "remains one of the last truly romantic experiences left on the mainline railway system in Britain".

Who could argue with that? With the future of sleeper travel between Scotland and London secure until at least 2029, David reasons that the cross-border route is arguably now more popular than ever.

This is a great read for those who have experienced travelling on a sleeper, and for those who have not, it might be just what you need to give it a try. GW

First published: 2018 by Amberley Publishing
Price: £15.99
ISBN: 978 1 4456 7232 8

TRAIN *TRAVELLER* **NEW ZEALAND**

A SCENIC EXTRAVAGANZA

THE RAILWAY LINE BETWEEN AUCKLAND AND WELLINGTON IN NEW ZEALAND IS LISTED UNDER THE INGLORIOUS TITLE OF THE 'NORTH ISLAND MAIN TRUNK LINE'. **GRAHAM WEST** DISCOVERED IT IS ANYTHING BUT INGLORIOUS.

AUCKLAND — PAPAKURA — HAMILTON — OTOROHANGA — TE KUITI — TAUMARUNUI

For some unfathomable reason, the 'Northern Explorer' line fails to achieve the same level of recognition enjoyed by its counterparts on New Zealand's South Island - 'The Coastal Pacific' and the 'TranzAlpine'. But a scenic blockbuster it is.

Discovering the delights of this 423-mile train journey was, ironically, more the outcome of ineptitude than good planning. My wife Jenny and I had made the decision to intercept our daughter's 12 month backpacking expedition to Australia by flying out to join her and spend some time exploring this antipodean outpost for ourselves. And, since we would have to endure a near 24-hour flight in each direction, why not take the opportunity to fly the extra 1,600 miles, between Australia and 'the land of the long white cloud', New Zealand?

To justify the additional expense, we reasoned that we could take the opportunity to look-up two friends who had emigrated to NZ and with whom I had worked in the UK eons earlier, so we added this to our itinerary. My ineptness arose when booking our flights; for some reason I had assumed they lived in the capital, Wellington. They live in Auckland!

TALE OF **TWO CITIES**

Unable to change our flights without considerable cost, we decided that once in Wellington we would hire a car, drive the 400 plus miles north to Auckland and then hire a campervan to complete our tour of the country; my reasoning being that this would be a good introduction to the delights of New Zealand. This proved to be the case, since driving in New Zealand can only be described as a delight, reminiscent of driving in the UK during the 60s and 70s - with the added extras of stunning scenery, little traffic on the roads and, as a confirmed petrol head, an ➡

LEFT | *Manganui O Te Viaduct with Mt Ruapehu in the background.*

TRAIN TRAVELLER NEW ZEALAND

ABOVE | *Auckland's 1076ft high Skytower soaring above the harbour and cityscape.* VISIT AUCKLAND

BELOW RIGHT | *Crossing the Hapuawhenua Viaduct.* KIWIRAIL

interesting and healthy scattering of early British car brands - many now extinct at home - but all in surprisingly good condition in New Zealand!

My bungled planning also created the opportunity for us to absorb the unique beauty of New Zealand's North Island between Auckland and Wellington; not once but four times, three by road and once by train, since our return flight was - you guessed it - from Wellington! As it turned out we would have happily made the same journey several more times - particularly on the train, such is the 'smorgasbord' of scenic splendour this fascinating country delivers.

Although not the capital, Auckland is the most populous urban area within New Zealand and is a modern, bustling city. It is also one of few cities in the world to have harbours located on each of two major oceans, with the central part of its urban area occupying a narrow isthmus between the huge Manukau harbour, which connects with the Tasman Sea west, and the Waitematā harbour, which connects with the South Pacific Ocean east. How greedy can you be?

Though it has a healthy scattering of high-rise buildings, the dominant feature downtown is the Skytower from which you can view the city centre, both oceans, both harbours (each hosting a sea of boats - symbolising Auckland's reputation as the 'City of Sails') and, underscoring the country's extremely volatile geological location, a backdrop of low-lying, rain forest covered hills peppered with 48 extinct (one hopes) volcanic cones.

> "We had no expectations for this trip but there was no disguising the fact that this was not going to be a fast 'intercity' journey."

DIVERSE REGIONS

Having renewed our acquaintance with our friends, we spent our time being awed by the sights of New Zealand's North Island (Te Ika-a-Māui) and the northern part of South Island (Te Waipounamu) in our hired campervan. The country is almost unique for having three complex climatic regions within its 1,000-mile length: from Alpine to

104 | TRAIN TRAVELLER

temperate in South Island, and temperate to semi-tropical in North Island. Our exploration was contained within the temperate zone of both islands and we can testify that within this zone not only does it rain a great deal, it can also get seriously cold, even in their late spring. We recall with a shudder, standing outside a mobile fish and chip wagon one evening in Picton, South Island, getting seriously soaked and wind-whipped; we could easily have been in West Yorkshire mid-February!

Sadly, the day arrived when our camper tour ended, and after returning it to its base our friends kindly drove us to Auckland's railway station in the early hours of the morning to board a train destined for Wellington. Predictably, New Zealand saved its best weather for our last full day in the country, as it was a bright, beautiful, sunny morning. We said our goodbyes and boarded the train that stood, unusually to British eyes, alongside the road at the station. We had no expectations for this trip but there was no disguising the fact that this was not going to be a fast 'intercity' journey - who was in a hurry?

New Zealand is a complex, geologically unstable, and seismically active region. Its topography makes it a challenging place to lay long, straight stretches of rail for any great distance. To overcome this, railway engineers adopted a narrow gauge (track width) of 3'6", giving them greater freedom of curvature necessary to negotiate the many turns imposed by the tricky terrain. As the crow flies, the distance between Auckland and Wellington is around 306 miles so it gives you some idea as to the added length taken up by the twists, turns and detours necessary for the railway to connect its two major cities.

THE OVERLANDER

The 'Overlander', as it was called at the time of our trip (it has since been upgraded and renamed 'The Northern Explorer'), was just four carriages long.

Notably shorter than those in the UK (although the Northern Explorer carriages are longer) they nevertheless featured large panoramic windows offering unrestricted views, coupled with extremely comfortable seating - reminiscent of the level of comfort once enjoyed by passengers on early versions of the UK's Inter City125.

To try and give a detailed account (even if I could remember it) of the variety of scenic treasures that were progressively revealed during the journey would bore everyone rigid, so I have reduced my commentary to a selection of highlights.

Hauled by a single diesel locomotive for the early part of the journey, 'The Overlander' drew away from the station at a gentle pace and made its way south through the suburbs as we settled down for what was going to be a 12 hour journey, travelling through four distinct geographical regions of North Island. Tourists and commuters alike clearly use the service as it made several stops during the journey where locals boarded and alighted - their wonderfully distinctive Kiwi accents giving away their origins.

The first stop was at Papakura, a community just 18 miles south of Auckland, where a party of golfers boarded the train on their way to a tournament in Hamilton, 52 miles down the line. Their presence was highlighted with a welcome infusion of enthusiastic bonhomie and hilarity - added to which they generously shared their sandwiches and cakes with other passengers in the carriage - us included.

This sector of the route crosses the Waikato plains and accompanies the Waikato River (New Zealand's longest river at 264 miles) in several stretches, as well as the main State Highway 1. The landscape reminded us of the English countryside with lush green rolling farmland, open views and fenced-in, grazing livestock. As we approached Hamilton a sense of *déjà vu* descended, which was unsurprising since we had already driven through it three times - although from the train it took on a unique perspective.

Leaving Hamilton behind, the line continued across the Waikato plains before arriving at Otorohanga, a small town that sits alongside the Waipa River in the northern part of the King Country; so named after colonial forces invaded the Waikato region in the 1860s. Otorohanga, (Maori for ➔

BELOW | *National Park on the Volcanic Plateau - with Mt Ngauruho in the centre that starred as Mount Doom in Lord of the Rings.* KIWIRAIL

TRAIN TRAVELLER NEW ZEALAND

ABOVE | *Mt Ruapehu from the observation car.* ROBIN HEYWORTH

BELOW | *The Raurimu Spiral. It looks like a model railway on a grand scale.* DUANE WILKINS

'food for a long journey') is officially classed as the Kiwiana town of New Zealand, Kiwiana meaning quirky items and cultural icons that contribute to a sense of nationhood. The town achieved international fame in 1986 when it changed its name, briefly, to Harrodsville in support of Henry Harrod, a restauranteur based in the town of Palmerston North (some 200 miles away). It was an act of protest against Mohamed Al Fayed, then owner of Harrods department store in London, who tried to force Henry to change the name of his restaurant. The locals proposed that every business in Otorohanga change their name to 'Harrods'. In the event the District Council supported the idea of the town changing its name to Harrodsville. Mohamed Al Fayed withdrew his threat after being lampooned by the press and the town reverted to its original name.

THE SPIRAL

As we drew away from Otorohanga the orderly patchwork of fields and farmland that spread into the haze slowly gave way to undulating, grass covered hills dotted with grazing sheep and occasional clusters of trees. In many ways the landscape is reminiscent of the Welsh Marches. The line, hitherto reasonably straight and flat, started to curve and climb gently as it threaded its way through the valleys. Ahead was the town of Te Kuiti, the last major town in the southern tip of the Waikato Plains before we reached the notorious Raurimu Spiral that climbs up to the North Island's volcanic central plateau.

Te Kuiti is the self-proclaimed sheep shearing capital of the world and hosts New Zealand's annual games where all things ovine, such as shearing contests, sheep races and much more, take place. It was also where the diesel locomotive that had hauled us from Auckland was uncoupled and replaced with an electric loco - more powerful and necessary for the climb up the Raurimu Spiral.

The hills were becoming more heavily wooded in places as we continued to climb. The Tongarino Forest Park

"This elevated landscape sits above the Pacific Ring of Fire and surrounds the western, southern, and eastern sectors of North Island's highest volcanic mountain range."

boundary was to our left as we passed through the town of Taumarunui before reaching the small community that sits at the foot of the Raurimu Spiral. I remember reading about the 'Spiral' in a book belonging to my father called *The World's Railways and How They Work*, it was published in 1947 and may have spawned my interest in railways.

Spirals are not unique in the railway world - Switzerland has several and there is also one in the Canadian Rockies, but they mostly go through the mountains via tunnels. The Raurimu Spiral was a brilliant solution since it was built almost entirely on the exterior of the mountainside and incorporates just two short tunnels that allow the tracks to overlap and wind around in an ascending circle, before exiting through two quarter-turns and a horseshoe bend. From the air it looks like a good model railway set. For the passenger it provides an engaging spectacle that enables

you to see where you have just travelled four times before reaching the top - or the bottom, depending on your heading!

If you have to book seats for your journey, and you have a choice, there is always the conundrum as to which side of the train to sit in order to enjoy the best view - particularly if you don't know from which side the best views will present themselves. As it happened, we did not need to book seats for this journey, and even better, it wasn't fully occupied so we were able to hop about, which was most welcome when the train was climbing the spiral.

RING OF FIRE

At the top of the spiral lies New Zealand's vast, brooding central volcanic plateau. This elevated landscape sits above the Pacific Ring of Fire and surrounds the western, southern, and eastern sectors of North Island's highest volcanic mountain range - part of the Tongariro National Park. The most northerly mountain, Mt. Tongariro is 6,490ft (1,978m) high, the central volcanic coned Mt. Ngauruhoe that starred as Mount Doom in the Lord of the Rings movie is 7,514ft (2,291m) high, and the highest and most southerly is the permanently snow-capped Mt. Ruapehu at 9,176ft (2,797m) high.

North of Mt. Tongariro and almost plumb centre of North Island is Lake Taupo, New Zealand's largest lake (238 sq miles) that shimmers in the caldera of the dormant Taupo volcano. This volcano is known to have erupted 28 times within the last 27,000 years and, some 26,500 years ago, was responsible for the world's largest known eruption within the past 70,000 years!

As we reached the plateau, the lush green grass sheathed hills and leafy woodlands we had been travelling through gave way to a flatter landscape, hidden under swathes of both industrially planted pines and natural woodland. On the far eastern horizon, glimpsed through occasional areas of open space between the trees, we could see the peaks of Ngauruhoe and Ruapehu. Traversing the western edge of the Tongariro National Park the line climbs steadily, attaining a height of 2,706ft (825m) above sea

level upon reaching National Park station - officially the highest operational station on North Island.

Leaving National Park, the line continues to skirt the western perimeter of the plateau and crosses the first of what is a series of viaducts that span some impressively deep ravines carved by rivers that flow down directly from Raupehu and the plateau. The tallest of these, the Makatote Viaduct, is 260ft (79m) tall with a span of 860ft (262m); it was also the second largest on-route. But it was the Hapuawhenua Viaduct that, again, brought back memories of another black and white photograph in my father's book. This was of the original Hapuawhenua Viaduct, a curved structure built with spindly, cross-braced iron trusses, with a steam locomotive hauling a train of carriages making its way across. ➔

ABOVE LEFT | *The impressive curve on the Hapuawhenua viaduct.* KIWIRAIL

ABOVE | *Papa Cliffs in the Rangitikei plains.* ROBIN HEYWORTH

TRAIN *TRAVELLER* | 107

TRAIN TRAVELLER NEW ZEALAND

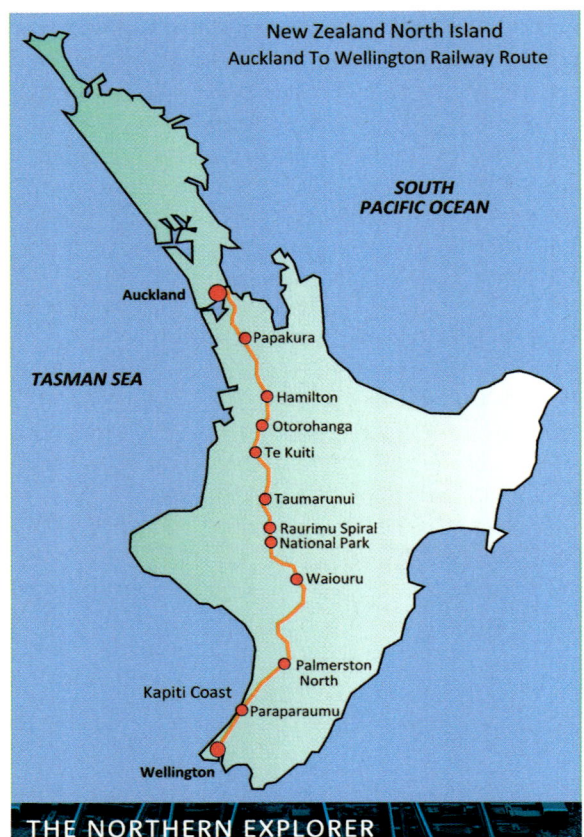

THE NORTHERN EXPLORER

Operator: KiwiRail - Great Journeys of New Zealand.
Web site: www.greatjourneysofnz.co.nz
Service: Formerly 'The Overlander' it has been upgraded and renamed 'The Northern Explorer'. This features longer, air-conditioned carriages with un-tinted, non-reflective panoramic side and roof windows, open deck observation areas. GPS enabled commentary in five languages, overhead information displays and a Café. The number of stops has also been reduced, knocking more than an hour off the original length of the journey.
Frequency: Auckland to Wellington: Monday, Wednesday, and Saturday.
Wellington to Auckland: Wednesday, Friday, and Sunday.
Distance: 423 miles. **Duration:** 11 hours.
Travel Option: Scenic Rail Pass offers unlimited travel on New Zealand's long-distance train network, including ferry travel between Wellington North Island and Picton, South Island.
Other Scenic Rail Journeys in New Zealand:
Coastal Pacific, South Island & TranzAlpine - all on South Island.
Summer Solstice: December 22
Winter Solstice: June 21
Currency: New Zealand Dollar

New Zealand's Northern Explorer was the focus of episode five in the second series of Channel 5's popular The World's Most Scenic Railway Journeys. Narrated by Bill Nighy, the series illustrates some of the best rail adventures that the planet has to offer. Catch it on Catchup.

This viaduct was replaced in 1987, by a new, elegant construction of tall, slim, concrete pillars that support the railway track some 167ft (51m) above a densely wooded valley. In the same year, a New Zealander known as Allan John 'A.J.' Hackett, made a bungy jump from the old viaduct, affirming in the process, the inhabitants' penchant for zany, questionable, dangerous pastimes. The old iron viaduct now forms part of the 'Old Coach Road' walking and cycling trail, a similar development to the Sustranscycle trails across the UK.

A little further down the line the route passes the small Maori community of Tangiwai, the site of New Zealand's worst rail disaster. On December 24, 1953, the Whangaehu River Bridge collapsed moments before the Wellington to Auckland passenger train was due to cross it - the locomotive and the first six carriages derailed into the river, killing 151 people. It was caused by the dam that held back Raupehu's volcanic crater lake giving way resulting in a 'lahar'; a violent flow of mud, slurry, rocky debris and water that washed down the river course destroying one of the bridge piers in its path.

RAGING RANGITIKEI

The next stop on the journey was at the small town of Waiouru. Sitting at an elevation of 2,598ft - just 108 feet lower than National Park - the landscape here switches dramatically to stark, flat, open, bush land, with unobscured views of Mt. Raupehu, and an area used extensively for training by New Zealand's army. From this point the train starts to descend, quite rapidly in places, as it leaves the plateau behind and heads into the Rangitikei region, an area that spreads southwest as far as Hawkes Bay in the Tasman Sea. The line originally crossed an area known as the Rangitikei plains, by following a narrow, tortuous route along the edges of the raging but beautiful Rangitikei River, another river flowing down from the central plateau. This river snakes its way along the foot of a long stretch of spectacular, sheer 'papa cliffs' a

Hunterville, a town famous for a dog known as Huntaways, a unique herding sheepdog that uses its bark to drive the flock. Shepherds travel here from all over New Zealand to enter the annual 'Shepherds Shemozzle' - an organised race for shepherds and their Huntaway dogs.

Hunterville was followed by Palmerston North, the country's seventh largest city, just 87 miles (141 km) north of Wellington. A giggle of schoolgirls, all smartly dressed in dark blue uniforms and mini bowler-style hats, boarded the train at Palmerston North Station, their enthusiastic chatter a delight to overhear. We had one more stop to make at Paraparaumu, a seaside town that lies on the Kapiti Coast, before arriving at Wellington. While we enjoyed this final and distinctively different stretch of our marathon journey, with the track hugging the edges of cliffs high above the ocean and passing through two long tunnels cut into the rocky terrain, it was marred by the growing realisation that the journey was coming to an end.

LEFT | *Crossing the Kawhatau River Bridge.* KIWI RAIL

BELOW | *Wellington's substantial neo-Georgian station.*

construct of soft, grey mudstone deposited on the sea floor some 15 million years ago. With steep gradients, tight curves, narrow tunnels, and regular landslides, it was a costly route to maintain, so in 1987 New Zealand Railways realigned and upgraded this section of the line. Tagged the 'Rangitikei deviation' the revised route entailed building three new bridges to cross the river to achieve a workable and sustainable re-alignment - each requiring an elevated level of earthquake resistance. As the train slows to traverse these bridges, the views of the papa cliffs and the twisting, clear waters are simply amazing. Even more amazing is that people pay good money to soil their underclothes on the jet boat trips available through the gorges!

The route now enters hill-farming country; characterised by a panorama of verdant, lumpy hills that look like discarded woollen hats flecked with white sheep and clumps of native flora. Our next destination was

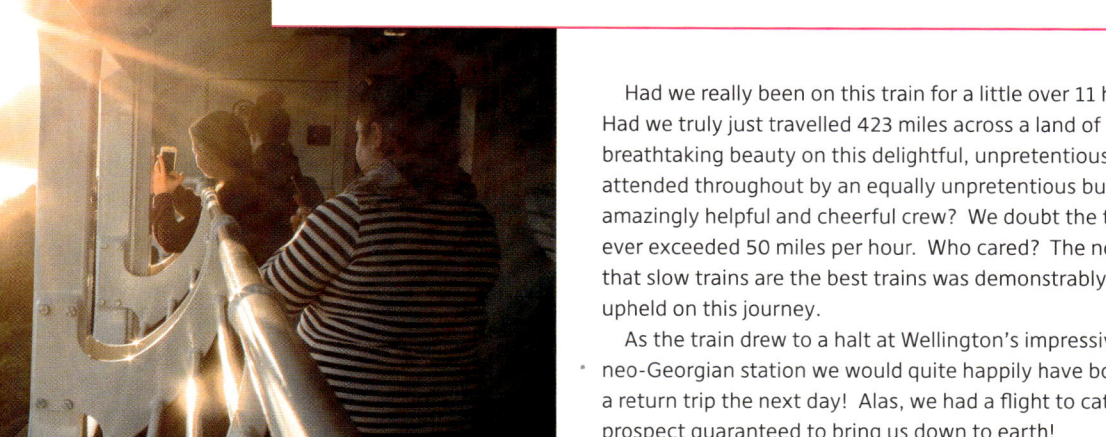

> "Had we truly just travelled 423 miles across a land of breathtaking beauty on this delightful, unpretentious train, attended by an equally unpretentious but amazingly helpful and cheerful crew?"

LEFT | *Hugging the Kapiti Coast just north of Wellington.* ROBIN HEYWORTH

Had we really been on this train for a little over 11 hours? Had we truly just travelled 423 miles across a land of breathtaking beauty on this delightful, unpretentious train, attended throughout by an equally unpretentious but amazingly helpful and cheerful crew? We doubt the train ever exceeded 50 miles per hour. Who cared? The notion that slow trains are the best trains was demonstrably upheld on this journey.

As the train drew to a halt at Wellington's impressive, neo-Georgian station we would quite happily have booked a return trip the next day! Alas, we had a flight to catch - a prospect guaranteed to bring us down to earth!

Admirationem autem stultitiam! (Out of folly comes wonderment)

TRAIN *TRAVELLER* *EXPERIENCE*

THE VIRTUES OF NOSTALGIA

REGULAR COMMUTERS BY TRAIN AND OCCASIONAL TRAIN TRAVELLERS MAY HAVE DIFFERING VIEWS ON THE RAIL EXPERIENCE. **MICHAEL WILLIAMS** HAS DONE MORE TRAIN TRAVELLING THAN MOST AND IS WELL PLACED TO TRY AND UNDERSTAND THE ROMANCE OF THE IRON ROAD.

Sometimes you come across a lofty railway viaduct, marooned in the middle of a remote country landscape. Or a crumbling platform of some once-bustling junction buried beneath the buddleia. If you are lucky, you might be able to follow some rusting tracks, or explore an old tunnel leading to…well, who knows where? Listen hard. Is that the wind in the undergrowth? Or the spectre of a train from the past panting up the embankment?

If you are a railway enthusiast, you will recognise the frisson of nostalgia that these images generate. We are fascinated by the romance of the past, as we see it – tales of lines prematurely axed, as well as marvels of locomotive engineering sent to the scrapyard before their time, and architecturally magnificent stations felled by the wrecker's ball. Then there are the lost delights of train travel, such as *haute cuisine* in the dining car, the grand expresses with their evocative names, and continental boat trains to romantic far-off places. Such pleasures have all but vanished in our modern homogenised era of train travel.

But why should nostalgia be on anyone's mind in this age of fast, state-of-the-art trains, that routinely whisk us efficiently all over the developed world at speeds of up to 200mph. Is it merely fanciful and indulgent to summon up some 'lost age' of the railways when more of us are choosing to use the modern rail network than at any time in history? Trains today, the mantra goes, are faster, more frequent, and better than ever. Why bother about the past?

Well for many of today's train travellers, 'faster, more frequent and better' is too often a euphemism, in corporate railway speak, for worse. It is sometimes tempting to wonder if deep in every railway operations HQ there is a department whose sole job is to think up ways of corroding the experience of passengers (or 'customer experience' if you go along with the jargon). Here are seats that don't line up with the windows, garish plasticky interiors, an incomprehensible fares system, ticket collectors who assume everyone is a criminal, a cacophony of endless announcements about the 'next station stop' and 'suspicious packages', and, of course, the extinction of many of the things that once made rail travel joyous – ➡

LEFT |
"Comfortable, dusty coaches rolling through the low woods, the sun gilding the green leaves."
PAUL THEROUX.
DENIS CHICK

TRAIN TRAVELLER EXPERIENCE

RIGHT | *'Obliging porters, staffed stations, waiting rooms with blazing fires...' Michael Williams. This restored waiting room on Great Central Railway's heritage Quorn and Woodhouse station is typical of many on the line that once connected London Marylebone with Manchester, Sheffield, Leicester, Loughborough, Brigg, Grimsby and Cleethorpes. Compare this with the image on page 114 of a 'modern' waiting room on Brigg station today!*
GREAT CENTRAL RAILWAY - QUORN & WOODHOUSE STATION COLLECTION

restaurant cars with starched tablecloths and silver service, obliging porters, staffed stations, waiting rooms with blazing fires, a comfy compartment you could snuggle in, luggage in advance...I'm sure you can devise your own list. No wonder the universe of railways of the past seems rose tinted.

But let us not get too carried away. There are many tangible things we have lost over the years that it would be unreasonable to expect to recover in the modern age. Nor would we want them. That romantic little branch line train was often as illusory as George Orwell's 'old maids bicycling to holy communion through the morning mist'. As Paul Theroux wrote in the early 1980s: "There is an English dream of a warm summer evening on a branch line train. Just that sentence can make an English person over 40 fall silent with the memory of what has now become a golden fantasy of an idealised England: the comfortable, dusty coaches rolling through the low woods, the sun gilding the green leaves and striking through the carriage windows; the breeze tickling the hot flowers in the fields, birdsong and the thump of the powerful locomotive; the pleasant creak of the wood panelling on the coach; the mingled smell of fresh grass and coal smoke; and the expectation of being met by someone very dear on the platform of a country station."

The reality was often that the train was a draughty, superannuated relic, fit only for the scrapyard, used by a handful of passengers each week, and leaching a bottomless pit of money from the public purse. No one could expect to revive it.

Likewise, present-day 'railwayacs' and 'locoists' wax sentimental about the colourful liveries and polished brass work of the steam engines of yore. We may enthuse about the 'Blackberry Black' of the London & North Western at Euston or the 'Improved Engine Green' of the London Brighton & South Coast Railway (which was actually yellow) – much as a design guru might fuss over a Farrow & Ball paint card. Yet the truth is, lovely though they seem in retrospect, they were labour-intensive and inefficient machines and by the 1950s, it became difficult to attract staff to work with them. To recreate any part of this world would be absurd today.

Yet most of us British, I think, cannot help but view the railways through a prism of nostalgia. The mood seems to be everywhere. Here is Michael Portillo, ubiquitous on our living room TVs, brandishing his Bradshaw and endlessly roaming the rails and catching the zeitgeist with his *Great Train Journeys*. Pete Waterman is there, too, rejoicing in the greasy world of the steam engine, while Tony Robinson adds the gloss of the celebrity historian.

So, what is it about trains that makes us so rheumy-eyed? Is it that, as the nation that invented the railway, we are pining in a post-modern world for our lost industrial heritage? In the introduction to their anthology *Train Songs*, the poets Sean O'Brien and Don Paterson reckon that the appeal of the railways is precisely to do with their relationship to time. "The train moves into the future on its iron road while provoking a complex nostalgia that has accompanied it since birth," they write. "Almost as soon as the railway arrived in Britain it began to depart. After the railway boom of the 1840s the empire of the tracks seems always to have been defending and withdrawing from its own frontiers…"

A cocktail of loss stirred with the recall of vanished pleasure is ever present in the literature of rail travel – moments fleetingly experienced and then lost forever. Here is Auden's *Night Mail* ever hurrying on with "letters of thanks, letters from banks, letters of joy from girl and boy". For Edward Thomas it was the sublime moment when his express train paused at Adlestrop and "for that minute a blackbird sang". Philip Larkin peeks from a train momentarily into the romantic lives of strangers in *Whitsun Weddings*. For Thomas Hardy life is never the same after a snatched kiss at the barrier in *On the Departure Platform*. "Each a glimpse and gone forever!" as Robert Louis Stevenson puts it in his famous *From a Railway Carriage*.

Much more than merely agents of commerce and industry, we love the railways because they encapsulate the whole gamut of human life and experience. They are the focus of emotions and the stuff of memories. The railway station, observe the social historians Jeffrey Richards and John M. Mackenzie, is a gateway through which people pass "in profusion on a variety of missions – a place of motion and emotion, arrival and sorrow, parting and reunion". It is a place of "countless stories" – of drama, mystery, and adventure.

Yet many of these stories belong to a world long gone – lyrically described by Gilbert and David St John Thomas in their charming book *Double-Headed*: "Railways are in a world of their own; they are segregated from the rest of the nation, and yet they serve it. They are self-contained, definable, understandable even by attentive amateurs and therefore welcoming to escapists; yet they are ubiquitous, infinitely diverse, complex within their own limits and wrapped in their own mystique. They have their own language, their own telephone network, their eating houses, factories and estates; they have their own slums, palaces, mausoleums and rustic beauty; they offer majesty and meanness, laughter, wonder and tears."

Not much of this could be said of the railways of today. It is hardly surprising, then, that we should invest so much emotion in romantic nostalgia. Who could disagree with that most poetic of railway historians Cuthbert Hamilton Ellis when he wrote (in 1947): "Surely it was always summer when we made our first railway journeys? Only from later boyhood do we remember what fog was like at Liverpool Street… or how the Thames Valley looked between Didcot and Oxford when there was naught but steel-grey water upon the drowned meadows. No, it was always summer! Sun shone on the first blue engine to be seen, a Somerset & Dorset near Poole; there was sunshine most dazzling on a Great Western brass dome; the sun shone on an extraordinary mustard-coloured engine of the London, Brighton & South Coast." "Nostalgic?" asks Hamilton Ellis. "If so, why not?"

And why not, indeed? This sense of what the railways of the past signify to us has been heightened recently by the renaissance of railway enthusiasm. Gone are the days

LEFT | *'…restaurant cars with starched tablecloths and silver service…' Michael Williams.* S J TAYLOR / GREAT CENTRAL RAILWAY

TRAIN TRAVELLER EXPERIENCE

ABOVE | *Brigg Station passenger shelter today. Reduced to just three seats!*
G WEST

when those with an interest in railways were derided as train spotters, anoraks, or rivet counters, and mocked in the routine of almost every second-rate comedian on the stand-up circuit. The mark of respectability came in autumn 2014 when the National Railway Museum staged an exhibition called *Trainspotting,* in which various celebrities 'came out' to declare their interest in what 20 years ago might have been an unspeakable taboo.

Actually, railway enthusiasm never really went away and – despite the mockers – has a long and noble history. The first railway enthusiast can be reckoned to be the 21-year-old actress Fanny Kemble who in 1830, just before the opening of the Liverpool & Manchester Railway, charmed George Stephenson into letting her ride with him on the locomotive. The engine, she gasped, was "a magical machine, with its flying white breath and rhythmical, unvarying pace." Recognition of what was to become a national pursuit initially came when Stephenson's 1825 engine *Locomotion* was put on public display on a plinth at Darlington station in 1857. Soon, upright professional men indulged their hobby in a manner not dissimilar to butterfly collecting or philately. By the turn of the century they had their own magazine and their own club in London, the Railway Club – as smart a place to be in its own way as the Garrick or the Oxford & Cambridge.

Before its decline into unfashionability in the 1980s, trainspotting had become a national cult in which men and boys turned out in all weathers on platforms all over the land, accompanied by their 'Bible' – a well-thumbed copy of the Ian Allan *Locospotters' Guide.* I recall having to fight my way to the end of the platform at King's Cross and Paddington through throngs of boys with notebooks and lapels plastered with enamel badges of their favourite engines. Then we discovered Pink Floyd and girls – and all grew up.

These days things have come full circle, with wealthy hedge fund managers in the City indulging their baby-boomer passions by spending millions buying and restoring vintage express steam locomotives to run on the main line – motivated not by profit, but by the sheer joy of the thing. This is not surprising, since railway enthusiasm is the ultimate nostalgia in the imagination of what Orwell called a "nation of collectors." And why should such pleasures have to be defended? As the historian Roger Lloyd wrote in his book *The Fascination of Railways*: "I have never met a lover of railways who felt the slightest need to produce any justification for his pleasure. Why should he?" The NRM even had the confidence to commission some verse from the poet Ian McMillan giving trainspotting a modern family feel:

It's a life filled with moments that ring like a bell,
With elation the thrill of the chase;
It's a smile from your dad that says 'Yes, all is well
As he matches the grin on your face.
This is a hobby that never will pall.
Tomorrow's a spotting day. Well, aren't they all?

But, in 2020, is railway nostalgia more than just indulgent whimsy? It is certainly true that compared with the 'good old days' there is so much that is better about the modern railway. As I write this, sitting in front of me is the *ABC Railway Guide* from February 1953, with its well-worn buff cover and adverts for Lemon Hart Rum and *Punch* magazine – as familiar in the homes of our parents, as an old bible or prayer book. We may regret its passing, yet it paints a dismal picture of the train services of even the recent past. Back then, a railway journey from London to Manchester, for example, took around four hours with gaps of up to two hours between trains. Today, – or at least in normal times – there are three trains every hour taking half the time. Name almost any journey on the main lines of Britain and the story is mostly the same.

As well as being faster, today's trains are infinitely safer and cleaner, too – air conditioning rather than smuts in the eye. Even the remotest branch lines have it better, with regular timetables, and no more wondering when the train will come on a windswept platform in the middle of nowhere. Electronic information is ubiquitous – and if you fancy it, all today's train companies have real-time train information on their websites and apps, as well as twitter feeds. The world defined by the *ABC Railway Guide* is already in the trash.

For all this, though, we may wonder if in 50 years' time, we would ever be able to speak lovingly of today's railways with the warmth of Hamilton Ellis in the concluding words of *The Trains We Loved*: "These were the trains we loved; grand, elegant and full of grace. We knew them and they belonged to the days when we first gazed on the magic of cloud shadows sweeping over the Downs, when we first became fully aware of the smell of a Wiltshire village after rain, or when we first saw a Scottish mountain framed in a double rainbow so vivid that no painter dared to try to record it…They were the days when the steam locomotive, unchallenged, bestrode the world like a friendly giant."

MICHAEL WILLIAMS *is the best-selling author of On the Slow Train, On the Slow Train Again, Steaming to Victory and The Trains Now Departed. Michael is a journalist and academic – writing, broadcasting, and blogging on transport, society, the media, and other issues of the day for the national media and many other outlets. Michael is also a leading travel writer, reporting on journeys around the world for a variety of publications.*

Michael Williams's book 'The Trains now Departed: Sixteen journeys into the lost delights of Britain's railways' is published by Penguin, price £10.99